COLLINS

LINE DANCING

Áine Quinn

HarperCollins*Publishers*

All attempts have been made by the Publishers to contact and credit the owners of copyright material used in this book. In the event of any oversight, the Publisher will be glad to rectify in future editions any omissions notified to them.

HarperCollins Publishers
PO Box, Glasgow G4 0NB

First published 1997

Reprint 10 9 8 7 6 5 4 3 2 1 0

ISBN 0 00 472149 7

A catalogue record for this book is available from the British Library

Printed and bound in Great Britain by
Caledonian International Book Manufacturing, Glasgow

☆ *Contents* ☆

Contents

Advanced Level Dances

☆ Acknowledgements ☆

I am indebted to the many hundreds of dancers who have attended my classes. It has been a tremendous learning experience for me and has enabled me to compile this collection of dances. I also extend my thanks to the numerous choreographers from around the world who have kindly granted permission for me to feature their work here.

I wish to thank my husband Tom and our children Bronagh, Brèanainn and Doireann for their continued support. Also, my mother Kathleen and mother-in-law Eileen who are always available to take my place in the home.

My thanks to Gerry Callan of Sunshine Radio for his enthusiastic help and great knowledge of country music.

Finally, thank you to my wonderful troupe of demonstrators, Raymond Moan, Donna Bailey, Ada Mullen, Annette Mhic Ardail, Deirdre Robinson, Nuala Kennedy and Toirèasa Quinn, for their hard work and dedication to 'getting it right'.

An extra special thanks to Toirèasa who is equally at home on the computer, her secretarial skills have been invaluable.

This book is dedicated to my late father, Ruairì Ò Cinnèide, who passed on his great love of music and dance and encouraged me to make the most of my talents

Áine Quinn
Dundalk, 1997

☆ Line Dance Terminology ☆

a.k.a. An abbreviation standing for 'also known as', indicating an commonly used alternative term or title.

and Half of a COUNT or a quick count. That is, 'one-and-two' or 'and one-two'. Noted in cue sheets with an ampersand (&).

applejack A movement in which the weight is centered on the heel of one foot and the toe of the other (beginning in the CLOSE POSITION). It is danced with a slight side movement and as both knees bend slightly, the toes split apart. Also known as ***fancy feet.***

ball change A shifting of weight from the ball of one foot to the ball of the other foot. It usually is done as part of a KICK-BALL-CHANGE.

beat The beat is a series of sounds that make up music. Therefore, the beat is the unit of musical rhythm. Also known as ***count.***

boot hook See HOOK.

brush A front-to-back sweeping or scuffing movement of one foot against the floor while the other supports your body weight. Also known as ***scoop*** or ***scuff.***

butterfly See PIGEON TOES.

centre The dancer's balancing point in proper alignment. See also CLOSE POSITION.

cha-cha A Latin dance step, comprising five steps to four beats of music. Beginning with either the left or right foot, two steps are followed by a triple step.The rhythm is slow-slow-quick-quick-slow. Also known as a ***three-step pattern.*** See SHUFFLE.

charleston A four-step pattern in four beats of music:
1. Step right foot forward;
2. Kick left foot forward;
3. Step left foot back;
4. Touch right toe back.

Also known as ***charleston step*** or ***charleston kick.***

chasse A sliding movement to the side, i.e. step-close, step-close, step. The free foot never passes the supporting foot. Also know as ***gallop*** or ***sashay***.

chug See SCOOT.

chug turn See PADDLE TURN.

close To bring the feet together.

close position The position in which both feet are together under the centre of the body, heels together, toes together. Also known as the ***first position*** or ***starting position***.

coaster step Three steps in two beats of music (1 & 2) danced on the spot, i.e. step back, feet together (changing weight), step forward.

count See BEAT.

country strut See HEEL STRUT.

cross One foot moves across in front or behind the other

crossing shuffles See SAILOR STEP.

crossing triples See SAILOR STEP.

diagonal A movement left or right at 45° from centre, facing one wall

dig Touching the ball or heel of the non-supporting foot with a strong emphasis

dip A slight bend of the supporting knee, keeping the other knee straight

drag To bring the free foot slowly together to the supporting foot. Also known as ***draw*** or ***slide***.

draw See DRAG.

drunken sailor step One foot crosses slightly in front of the other while walking forward. Also known as ***drunken sailor walk***.

duck walk See HEEL STRUT.

first position See CLOSE POSITION.

fan This is a two-count movement, of which there are two varieties. To do a ***heel fan***, start with your feet in CLOSED POSITION, swing one heel out, then return to centre. For a ***toe fan***, start with feet in closed position then move the toe of one foot outward to one side and back to centre.

fast heel touches See HOP CHANGE.

grapevine A four-step movement in four beats travelling to the left or right.
1. Step to the side with one foot;
2. Step behind with the other foot;
3. Step to the side again with the first foot;
4. The final step can be a BRUSH, KICK, SCOOT, STOMP or TOUCH.

Also known as ***vine***. See also WEAVE.

grind A two-count movement: dig your heel into the floor, twisting your foot from centre outwards.

half turn A 180° turn to the left or right performed in two beats of music: step forward turn away from the forward foot to face the opposite direction, changing weight to the other foot.

heel Tap the floor with the heel of the foot, usually in front of the body

heel crashes See TOE STRUTS.

heel pivot A turn on the heel of one foot with no weight change

heel shifts With weight on balls of feet, a twisting action to the left or right with both heels.

heel splits See PIGEON TOES.

heel strut A two-count walk travelling forward. The heel contacts the floor first, then the whole foot flattens. Also known as ***strut***, ***country strut***, and ***duck walk***.

heel-toe walks See HEEL STRUTS.

heel touches See HOP CHANGE.

hip bump Rocking the hips to one side is referred to as hip bumps. The hips are rocked by keeping one knee stiff and bending the opposite knee.

hitch Lifting of your leg at the knee 90° angle from the floor

hitch-kick See KICK-BALL-CHANGE.

hitch turn HITCH and TURN together using hitch momentum to turn.

hold Remaining in position with no movement for a designated number of beats before taking the next step. Also known as ***pause***.

hook One foot crosses either in front or behind the supporting leg between the knee and the ankle. Also known as ***boot hook***.

hook turn See SPIN.

hop A jump off the floor in any direction without switching weight to the other foot

hop change Begin with one heel forward: in one beat, hop and switch to the other heel forward. Also known as ***heel switches***, ***fast heel touches***, ***Mexican heels***, ***Mexican hat dance***.

jazz box A four-count step performed by:
1. Crossing one foot over the other;
2. Step back on the other foot;
3. Step the first foot to the side;
4. Close.

Also known as ***jazz square***.

jump A jump off the floor landing on both feet.

jumping jack A jump off the floor landing on both feet diagonally apart with one heel extended forward.

kick A quick foot movement in the air with no weight change. Generally a kick comes out from the knee, not the hip.

kick-ball-change A three-step pattern in two beats:
1. Kick forward;
& Step on the ball of the same foot centred under the body (1&);
2. Step on second foot beside first.

lock A tight cross of the feet.

Mexican hat dance See HOP CHANGE.

Mexican heels See HOP CHANGE.

Monterey turn A four-count HALF TURN (180°):
1. Touch right toe to right side;
2. Turn one half to the right on the left foot, bringing the right foot to the left foot, switching weight;
3. Touch left toe to left side;
4. Close.
Also known as ***Monterey spin***.

over To step across the supporting foot.

paddle turn A half, three-quarter or full turn, shifting the weight from one foot to the other. Push with one foot and pivot on the other. Also know as ***chug turn***.

pause See HOLD.

pigeon toes A two-count movement. With your feet in the CLOSED POSITION, and your weight on the balls of both feet
1. Spread heels apart;
2. Bring heels together.
Also known as ***butterfly***, ***buttermilk***, ***heel splits*** and ***splits.***

pivot or **pivot turn** See HALF TURN.

point A toe TOUCH to the front, side or back; the body is supported by the non-pointing foot.

polka Similar to a SHUFFLE but done in a more lively style.

quarter turn A 90° turn to the left or right

rock or rock step Shifting the weight from one foot to the other. The type of rock step is determined by the first step, e.g. rock forward, rock back, etc.

sailor step A three-step pattern in two beats. It is similar to a SHUFFLE, except that the foot crosses over on the first step. Also known as ***crossing triples*** and ***crossing shuffles***.

sailor shuffles A three-step movement in two beats (1&2). The emphasis is on the last step.
1. Step one foot behind;
& Step on the ball of the other foot to the side;
2. Step the first foot to the side with full body weight to emphasise the movement.
Also known as ***vaudeville step***.

scissors A series of CROSS OVER steps in various combinations in syncopated rhythm. See also TOE SPLITS.

scoot A forward movement of one foot while the other foot is hitched (lifted) off the floor. The scooting foot remains in contact with the floor (do not hop). Also known as ***chug***.

scoop See BRUSH.

scuff See BRUSH.

shimmy To shake the shoulders and upper body.

shuffle A three-step movement in two beats (1 & 2) which can be done in any direction: forward, backward, sideways or diagonal.
1. Step on one foot in desired direction;
& Step second foot beside first (on ball of foot);
2. Step first foot in same direction again.The second foot never passes the first.
Also known as ***cha-cha***, ***polka***, and ***triple step***.

slide See DRAG.

star A series of point movements in which the toe is pointed to the front, side and back or in reverse

starting position See CLOSE POSITION.

step Placing the foot in any position taking weight.

stomp Hitting the floor with the whole foot to make a noise. There is no change of weight to the stomping foot unless otherwise stated.

strut See HEEL STRUT.

styling Body movements that are not described for you on the cue sheet. It is the personal expression that you give to the dance and is very individual. Relax and let your body do the rest

swing Raise the free foot and move forward, backward, to the side or cross-wis.e

switch A quick shift of weight from one foot to the other. Normally done with a heel. See HOP CHANGE.

swivel Feet are in CLOSED POSITION. Rotate on balls of both feet. Also known as ***twist***.

syncopated steps A series of steps often described as 'double time'. Count 1 & 2 & 3 & 4 & . There is a movement on every BEAT and every half beat.

tap The toe of the free foot taps or touches the floor without a weight change.

tempo The speed of the beat of music, described in beats per minute (BPM).

toe fan See FAN.

toe splits See SCISSORS.

toe strut A two count walk travelling forward or backward. The ball of the foot contacts the floor first, followed by the heel. Also known as ***heel crashes***.

together Bring feet together with weight evenly distributed on both feet. Also known as ***close position*** or ***starting position***.

touch The foot touches the floor without a weight change.

travelling grapevine See WEAVE.

triple step See SHUFFLE.

turn A rotation of the body, taking one or more steps to complete.

twist See SWIVEL.

variation Movements of footwork that vary from the indicated dance patterns.

vaudeville step See SAILOR SHUFFLE.

vine See GRAPEVINE.

wall A wall refers to the direction of a line dance. There are four walls. and a line dance will be descibed as either be a 1-, 2- or 4-wall dance, indicating the number of changes in direction that will be made in the course of the dance.

weave A continuous GRAPEVINE of eight or more counts. Also known as ***travelling grapevine***.

weight change Shifting of body weight from one foot to the other.

☆ Notes on Symbols ☆

For each dance description, the following symbols are used as a quick visual guide to changes in direction as the dance progresses:

○ Dance on the spot

⇧	Move forward	⇨	Move to the right
⇩	Move back	⇦	Move to the left
⬀	Move forward diagonally to the right	⬂	Move backward diagonally to the right
⬁	Move forward diagonally to the left	⬃	Move backward diagonally to the left
●	Full turn on the spot	◕	Three-quarter turn to the left
◥	Quarter turn to the right	◗	Half turn to the right
◤	Quarter turn to the left	◖	Half turn to the left

The symbols are positioned against the instruction line at which the change takes place. There are also references to 'clock' positions (e.g. turns to 3 o'clock, to 6 o'clock, etc.) as an additional quick guide to particular movements. These assume that the 12 0'clock position is directly in front of you.

'&' Symbol
The appearance of this symbol indicates an extra step must be done in a beat of the music. So, for example, '17&18' indicates that there are three moves to be made during beats 17 and 18.

Beginner Level Dances

☆☆☆☆☆

☆☆☆☆☆ Back in Trouble ☆☆☆☆☆

Vera Brown, Campton, USA — ***Four Wall***

Beats	Movement	Direction
	Slow Walk	
1	Touch right toe forward	⇧
2	Drop right heel to floor	
3	Touch left toe forward	
4	Drop left heel to floor	
	Kick-Ball-Cross	
5	Kick right foot forward	⇨
&	Quickly step right foot next to left	
6	Cross left foot over right	
7	Step right foot to right	
8	Touch left foot next to left	
	Left Side Touches	
9	Touch left toe to left side	○
10	Touch left toe next to right foot	
11	Touch left toe to left side	
12	Touch left toe next to right foot	
	Kick-Ball-Cross	
13	Kick left foot forward	⇦
&	Quickly step left foot next to right	
14	Cross right foot over left	

(Contd.)

Beats	Movement	Direction
15	Step left foot to left side	⇦
16	Touch right foot next to left	
	Right Side Touches	
17	Touch right toe to right side	❍
18	Touch right toe next to left foot	
19	Touch right toe to right side	
20	Touch right toe next to left foot	
	Quarter Turn	
21	Step forward on right foot	
22	Step left foot in place making quarter turn to left	◖
	Stomps	
23	Stomp right foot next to left, shifting weight onto right foot	❍
24	Stomp left foot next to right, shifting weight onto left foot	
	Strolls	
25	Step right foot forward	⇧
26	Bring left foot up behind right leg, shift weight to left foot	
27	Step right foot forward	
28	Brush forward with left foot	
29	Step left foot forward	

Beats	Movement	Direction
30	Bring right foot up behind left leg, shift weight to right foot	⇧
31	Step left foot forward	
32	Brush right foot forward	

Begin again!

☆☆☆ Badly Bent Charleston ☆☆☆

Dee Belsher, Westminster, USA — ***Four Wall***

Beats	Movement	Direction
	Rock Steps	
1	Step right foot to right	⇨
2	Rock step on left foot behind right	
3	Step right foot in place	
4	Hold	
5	Step left foot to left	⇦
6	Rock step on right foot behind left	
7	Step left foot in place	
8	Hold	
9	Touch right toes over left foot	
10	Lower right heel, shift weight to right foot	⇩
11	Touch left toes back	
12	Lower left heel, shift weight to left	
13	Touch right toes back	
14	Lower right heel, shift weight to right foot	
15	Touch left toes over right foot	
16	Lower left heel, shift weight to left	
	Vine Right	
17	Step right foot to right	⇨

Beats	Movement	Direction
18	Cross left foot behind right	
19	Step right foot to right	⇨
20	Kick left foot forward and clap	
	Vine Left	
21	Step left foot to left	⇦
22	Cross right foot behind left	
23	Step left foot to left	
24	Kick right foot forward and clap	
	Charleston	
25	Step right foot forward	❍
26	Kick left foot forward and clap	
27	Step left foot back	
28	Touch right toes back and clap	
	Charleston with Quarter Turn	
29	Step right foot forward, making quarter turn to right	◗
30	Kick left foot forward and clap	
31	Step left foot back	
32	Touch right toes back and clap	

Begin again!

☆☆☆☆☆ Belt Buckle Boogie ☆☆☆☆☆

Jen Cumming, Peterborough, Canada — ***Two Wall***

Beats	Movement	Direction
1,2	With weight on balls of feet, tap heels on floor twice	○
	Vines	
3	Step to right on right foot	⇨
4	Cross left foot behind right	
5	Step to right on right foot	
6	Hitch left knee (raise it)	
7	Step to left on left foot	⇦
8	Cross right foot behind left	
9	Step to left on left foot	
10	Hitch right knee (raise it)	
	Hip Circles	
11	Step forward slightly on right foot and roll right hip forward, shifting weight onto right foot	○
12	Roll left hip back, shifting weight onto left foot	
13	Roll right hip forward, shifting weight onto right foot	
14	Roll left hip back, shifting weight onto left foot	

Beats	Movement	Direction
	Triple-steps and Rock Turn	
15&16	Triple-step forward starting with right foot (right, left, right)	⇧
17	Step forward on left foot	
18	Rock back on right foot, beginning half turn to left	◖
19&20	Complete left turn with a triple-step, starting with left foot (left, right, left)	⇧
21	Step forward on right foot	
22	Step in place on left foot	○
23	Step back on right foot	
24	Step in place on left foot	
	Double Bumps	
25, 26	Step forward on right foot and bump right hip forward twice	⇧
27, 28	Step forward on left foot and bump left hip forward twice	
	Quarter Turns	
29	Step forward on right foot	
30	Make quarter turn to left, shifting weight to left foot	◔
31	Step forward on right foot	
32	Make quarter turn to left, shifting weight to left foot	◔

(Contd.)

Beats	Movement	Direction
	Stomps and Spread Cross Turn	
33	Stomp right foot and put weight on it	○
34	Stomp left foot and put weight on both feet	
35	Jump up and land with feet apart	
36	Jump up and land with right foot in front of left	
37	Unwind legs, making half turn to left	◖
38	Clap	

Begin again!

☆☆☆☆☆☆☆ *Bubba 2* ☆☆☆☆☆☆☆

Four Wall

Beats	Movement	Direction
	Heel Taps and Swivels	
1	Tap right heel forward	❍
2	Step right foot beside left	
3	Swivel heels right	
4	Swivel heels left	
5	Swivel heels right	
6	Swivel heels centre	
	Hook and Swivels	
7,8	Repeat steps 1,2	❍
9	Tap right heel forward	
10	Hook right foot across left shin	
11	Tap right heel forward	
12	Step right foot beside left	
13–16	Repeat steps 3–6	
	Hook and Diagonal Steps	
17	Tap left heel forward	❍
18	Hook left foot across right shin	
19,20	Repeat steps 17,18	
21	Step left foot forward diagonally	
22	Stomp right foot beside left	
23	Step right foot back to place	

(Contd.)

Beats	Movement	Direction
24	Stomp left foot beside right	❍
25–28	Repeat steps 21–24	
29	Step left foot forward turning quarter turn to left	◖
30	Stomp right foot beside left *(no weight on stomp)*	
31	Step right foot back	⇩
32	Step left foot back	
33,34	Stomp right foot beside left twice *(no weight on stomp)*	

Begin again!

☆☆☆ Chocolate City Hustle ☆☆☆

Four Wall

Beats	Movement	Direction
	Walk Forward and Backward	
1	Step right foot forward	⇧
2	Step left foot forward	
3	Step right foot forward	
4	Scuff left foot forward	
5	Step left foot back	⇩
6	Step right foot back	
7	Step left foot back	
8	Scuff right foot forward	
	Right and Left Vine	
9	Step right foot to right side	⇨
10	Step left foot behind right	
11	Step right foot to right side	
12	Touch left foot beside right	
13	Step left foot to left side	⇦
14	Step right foot behind left	
15	Step left foot to left side	
16	Touch right foot beside left	
	Four Step Touches	
17	Step right foot diagonally forward	⬀
18	Touch left foot beside right	

(Contd.)

Beats	Movement	Direction
19	Step left foot back in place	⇙
20	Touch right foot beside left	
21	Step right foot to right side	⇨
22	Touch left foot beside right	
23	Step left foot to left side	⇦
24	Touch right foot beside left	
	Heel Swivels and Digs	
25	Swivel heels right	○
26	Swivel heels centre	
27	Swivel heels left	
28	Swivel heels centre	
29,30	Tap right heel forward twice	
31,32	Tap right toe behind twice	
33	Tap right heel forward	
34	Tap right toe behind	
35	Touch right toe to right side	
36	Pivot quarter turn left on left foot, kicking right foot behind left	◢

Begin again!

☆ C. M. T. Jammin' Country Strut ☆

Jo Thompson, Nashville, USA **_Four Wall_**

Beats	Movement	Direction
	Toe Struts and Knee Pops	
1	Step right foot forward on ball of foot	⇧
2	Slap right heel down	
3	Step left foot forward on ball of foot	
4	Slap left heel down	
5,6	Kick right foot forward, twice	
7&	Step right foot back *(bend left knee and raise heel)*	
8	Step left heel down *(raise right heel)*	
9–16	Repeat steps 1–8	⇧
	Rock Steps, Stomps and Heel Clicks	
17	Rock forward onto right foot	❍
18	Rock back onto left foot	
19	Rock back onto right foot	
20	Rock forward onto left foot	
21	Stomp right foot in place	❍
22	Stomp left foot in place	
23,24	Click heels together, twice (weight on balls of both feet)	❍

(Contd.)

Beats	Movement	Direction
	Side Shuffles and Rock	
25&26	Shuffle to right side, right, left, right	⇨
27	Rock forward onto left foot, crossing over right	
28	Rock back onto right foot	
29&30	Shuffle to left side, left, right, left	⇦
31	Rock forward onto right foot, crossing over left	
32	Rock back onto left foot	
	Unwinding Turn, Clap and Hip Bumps	
33	Step right foot to right side	
34	Cross left foot over right	
35, 36	Unwind three-quarter turn right *(weight on balls of both feet)* right foot will finish in front of left, with weight on left foot, and clap	◕
37,38	Bump hips forward, twice	○
39,40	Bump hips back, twice	
	Pivot Turns and Syncopated Jumps	
41	Step right foot forward	○
42	Pivot half turn left *(weight on balls of both feet)*	
43,44	Repeat steps 41,42	

Beats	Movement	Direction
&45	Jump forward on right foot, then left	⇧
46	Clap	
&47, 48	Repeat steps &45,46	

Begin again!

☆☆☆☆☆☆ Country Boy ☆☆☆☆☆☆

Four Wall

Beats	Movement	Direction
	Heel Digs	
1	Tap right heel forward	❍
2	Step right foot in place	
3	Tap left heel forward	
4	Step left foot in place	
5–8	Repeat steps 1–4	
	Double Digs	
9,10	Tap right heel forward, twice	❍
11,12	Tap right toe behind, twice	
	With weight on left foot, swivel left foot travelling to right	
13	Swivel toes right	⇨
14	Swivel heel right	
15	Swivel toes right	
16	Swivel heel right	
	At the same time, tap right foot slightly in front of left foot	
13	Heel to the floor, toes pointed out	⇨
14	Toes to the floor, heel pointed out	
15	Heel to the floor, toes pointed out	

Beats	Movement	Direction
16	Toes to the floor, heel pointed out	
	Heel Struts	
17	Step right heel forward	⇧
18	Slap right foot down	
19	Step left heel forward	
20	Slap left foot down	
21–24	Repeat steps 17–20	
	Jazz Box with Turn	
25	Cross right foot over left	
26	Step left foot back	
27	Step right foot forward, turning quarter turn right	◗
28	Step left foot beside right	
	Jazz Box in Place	
29	Cross right foot over left	❍
30	Step left foot back	
31	Step right foot to right side	
32	Step left foot beside right	

Begin again!

☆☆☆☆☆ Cowgirl Twist ☆☆☆☆☆

Four Wall

Beats	Movement	Direction
	Heel Struts Forward	
1	Step right heel forward	⇧
2	Step right foot down	
3	Step left heel forward	
4	Step left foot down	
5–8	Repeat steps 1–4	
	Walk Backward	
9	Step right foot back	⇩
10	Step left foot back	
11	Step right foot back	
12	Step left foot beside right	
	Travelling Heel Twists, Left and Right	
13	Twist heels left	⇦
14	Twist toes left	
15	Twist heels left	
16	Clap	
17	Twist heels right	⇨
18	Twist toes right	
19	Twist heels right	
20	Clap	

Beats	Movement	Direction
	Heel Twists	
21	Twist heels left	❍
22	Clap	
23	Twist heels right	
24	Clap	
25	Twist heels left	
26	Twist heels right	
27	Twist heels left	
28	Twist heels centre	
	Heel Turn	
29,30	Tap right heel forward, hold	◖
31,32	Turn quarter turn to left, hold	

Begin again!

☆☆☆☆☆☆ Earthquake ☆☆☆☆☆☆

Four Wall

Beats	Movement	Direction
	Walk Forward	
1	Step right foot forward	⇧
2	Step left foot forward	
3	Step right foot forward	
4	Half turn to left, kick left high and clap	◖
5	Step left foot forward	⇧
6	Step right foot forward	
7	Step left foot forward	
8	Quarter turn to right, kick right high and clap	◗
	Walk Backward	
9	Step right back	⇩
10	Step left back	
11	Step right back	
12	Touch left foot beside right	
	Toe, Heel Taps	
13,14	Tap left toe back twice	○
15,16	Tap left heel forward twice	
17	Tap left toe back	

Beats	Movement	Direction
18	Tap left heel forward	O
	Switch Feet	
&	Step left foot back	O
19	Tap right heel forward	
	Roll Hips	
20	Roll hips forward	O
21	Roll hips back	
22	Roll hips forward	
23	Roll hips back and draw right foot back	
24	Scuff right foot forward	
	Begin again!	

☆☆☆☆☆☆ Electric Slide ☆☆☆☆☆☆

Four Wall

Beats	Movement	Direction
	Right Vine	
1	Step right foot to right side	⇨
2	Step left foot behind right	
3	Step right foot to right side	
4	Stomp left foot beside right (no weight on stomp) *or* Scuff left heel next to right	
	Left Vine	
5	Step left foot to left side	⇦
6	Step right foot behind left	
7	Step left foot to left side	
8	Stomp right foot beside left (no weight on stomp) *or* Scuff right heel next to left	
	Walk Back	
9	Step back right	⇩
10	Step back left	
11	Step back right	
12	Touch left toes next to right (no weight on touch step)	

Beats	Movement	Direction
13	Step left foot forward	❍
14	Touch right toes next to left	
15	Step right foot back	
16	Touch left toes next to right	
17	Step left foot forward, with quarter turn to left	◖
18	Scuff right foot forward	

Begin again!

☆☆☆ The Florida Love Bug ☆☆☆

Louise G. Webber, Spring Hill, USA — **_Four Wall_**

A simple dance, ideal for beginners to learn some basic moves. More experienced dancers can use the opportunity to experiment. Try doing a turn during the grapevine r during the steps in place.

Beats	Movement	Direction
	Heel Taps	
1	Tap left heel forward	○
2	Tap left heel forward again	
3	Tap left toe back	
4	Tap left toe back again	
	Left Vine	
5	Step to left with left foot	⇦
6	Cross right foot behind left	
7	Step to left with left foot	
8	Stomp right foot	
9	Step to right with right foot	⇨
10	Slide left foot to meet right	
11&12	Step right, left, right in place	
13	Step to left with left foot	⇦
14	Slide right foot to meet left	
15&16	Step left, right, left in place	

Beats	Movement	Direction
	Heel Taps	
17	Tap right heel forward	○
18	Tap right heel forward again	
19	Tap right toe back	
20	Tap right toe back again	
	Right Vine	
21	Step to right with right foot	⇨
22	Cross left foot behind right	
23	Step to right with right foot	
24	Stomp left	
25	Step to left with left foot	⇦
26	Slide right foot to meet left	
27&28	Step left, right, left in place	
29	Step to right with right foot	⇨
30	Slide left foot to meet right	
31&32	Step right, left, right in place	
	Charleston	
33	Step forward on left foot	○
34	Kick right foot forward	
35	Step back on right foot	
36	Point left toes way back	

(Contd.)

Beats	Movement	Direction
	Charleston with Turn	
37	Step forward on left with quarter turn to left	◀
38	Kick right foot forward	
39	Step back on right foot	
40	Point left toes way back	

Begin again!

☆☆☆☆☆☆ The Freeze ☆☆☆☆☆☆

Four Wall

This is a short and simple dance with basic steps that are the foundation for many other line dances – great for beginners.

Beats	Movement	Direction
	Right Vine	
1	Step right foot to right side	⇨
2	Step left foot behind right	
3	Step right foot to right side	
4	Tap left foot beside right	
	Left Vine	
5	Step left foot to left side	⇦
6	Step right foot behind left	
7	Step left foot to left side	
8	Tap right foot beside left	
	Walk Backward	
9	Step right foot back	⇩
10	Step left foot back	
11	Step right foot back	
12	Hitch left foot (raise left knee)	
	Rock Steps, Scuff, Turn	
13	Rock (lean) forward onto left foot	❍

(Contd.)

Beats	Movement	Direction
14	Rock (lean) back onto right foot	❍
15	Rock (lean) forward onto left foot	
16	Scuff right foot forward, at the same time turn quarter turn left on left foot *(To scuff, hit right heel off the floor as you sweep right foot past left)*	◖

Begin again!

☆☆☆☆ God Blessed Texas ☆☆☆☆

Shirley Batson, USA — ***Two Wall***

Beats	Movement	Direction
	Diagonal Steps	
1	Step left foot forward diagonally	⇘
2	Stomp right foot beside left and clap	
3	Step right foot back to place	⇘
4	Stomp left foot beside right and clap	
5	Step left foot back diagonally	⇙
6	Stomp right foot beside left and clap	
7	Step right foot forward to place	⇗
8	Stomp left foot beside right and clap	
	Stomps and Knee Rolls	
9	Stomp left foot to left side	○
10	Stomp right foot to right side (feet now shoulder width apart)	
11	Place right hand on right thigh	
12	Place left hand on left thigh	
13,14	Roll right knee clockwise, twice	
15,16	Roll left knee counterclockwise, twice	
	Variation for Chorus Only	
13–16	Pump fists in air, right, left, right, left *(join with Little Texas and shout 'God Blessed Texas')*	

(Contd.)

Beats	Movement	Direction
	Right Vine	
17	Step right foot to right side	⇨
18	Step left foot behind right	
19	Step right foot to right side	
20	Touch left foot beside right	
	Left Vine	
21	Step left foot to left side	⇦
22	Step right foot behind left	
23	Step left foot to left side	
24	Touch right foot beside left	
	Hitches	
25	Step right foot forward	⇧
26	Hitch left (raise knee) turning half to right	◗
27	Hitch left again	
28	Step left foot forward	⇧
29	Hitch right	
30	Hitch right again	
31	Step right foot forward	
32	Hitch left	

Begin again!

☆☆☆☆ The Grundy Gallop ☆☆☆☆

Two Wall

Beats	Movement	Direction
	Circle Shuffles	
1–8	Complete a full circle counter-clockwise (left) in four shuffles: left shuffle, right shuffle, left shuffle, right shuffle *(each shuffle takes quarter of the circle)*	⇙ ⇖ ⇘ ⇗
	Toe Touches	
9	Touch left toe to left side	○
10	Step left foot beside right	
11	Touch right toe to right side	
12	Step right foot next to left	
	Heel, Toe, Shuffle Forward	
13	Touch left heel forward	⇧
14	Touch left toe back	
15&16	Shuffle forward, left, right, left	
17	Touch right heel forward	⇧
18	Touch right toe back	
19&20	Shuffle forward, right, left, right	

(Contd.)

Beats	Movement	Direction
	Step Forward, Rock Back, Shuffle Backward	
21	Step left foot forward	
22	Rock back onto right foot	
23&24	Shuffle backwards, left, right, left	⇩
	Step Back, Rock Forward, Shuffle Forward	
25	Step right foot back	
26	Rock forward onto left foot	
27&28	Shuffle forward, right, left, right	⇧
	Step, Turn, Stomp	
29	Step left foot forward	
30	Pivot half turn right (on balls of both feet)	◗
31	Stomp left foot in place	❍
32	Stomp right foot in place	

Begin again!

☆☆☆☆☆☆ Guitar Boogie ☆☆☆☆☆☆

Anne King, Atlanta, USA **Four Wall**

The '&' indicates an extra step in 2 beats, so in 17&18 and 19&20 there are 3 moves in 2 beats. A Paddle Turn (left foot stays in place as right foot steps around the outside) is described in steps 25–30.

Beats	Movement	Direction
	Vines with Turns	
1	Step right foot to right	⇨
2	Cross left foot behind right	
3	Step right foot to right	
4	Scuff left foot, making quarter turn to right	◔
5	Step left foot to left	⇦
6	Cross right foot behind left	
7	Step left foot to left, turning foot to left to begin turn	
8	Make three-quarter turn to left on ball of left foot	◕
	Toe-Heel Walk	
9	Touch right toe forward	⇧
10	Lower right heel to floor *(weight now on right foot)*	
11	Touch left toe forward	

(Contd.)

Beats	Movement	Direction
12	Lower left heel to floor	⇧
13–14	Repeat steps 9–10	
15–16	Repeat steps 11–12	
	Kick-Ball-Change	
17	Kick right foot forward	❍
&	Step right foot next to left	
18	Step left foot in place	
19	Kick right foot forward	❍
&	Step right foot next to left	
20	Step left foot in place	
	Jazz Box	
21	Cross right foot over left	❍
22	Step left foot back	
23	Step right foot to right	
24	Step left foot next to right	
	Paddle Turn	
25	Step right foot forward	
26	Make quarter turn to left, shifting weight back to left foot	◖
27	Step right foot forward	
28	Make quarter turn to left, shifting weight back to left foot	◖
29	Step right foot forward	

Beats	Movement	Direction
30	Make quarter turn to left, shifting weight back to left foot	◀
31	Rock forward on right foot	❍
32	Step left foot in place	

Begin again!

☆☆☆☆☆ Harpoon Stomp ☆☆☆☆☆

Carol Paulsen, Port Clyde, USA — ***Four Wall***

Beats	Movement	Direction
	Walk Forward	
1	Step right foot forward	⇧
2	Step left foot forward	
3	Step right foot forward	
4	Stomp left foot next to right *(do not put weight on left foot)*	
	Walk Backward	
5	Step left foot back	⇩
6	Step right foot back	
7	Step left foot back	
8	Stomp right foot next to left *(do not put weight on right foot)*	
	Vine Right	
9	Step right foot to right	⇨
10	Cross left foot behind right	
11	Step right foot to right	
12	Stomp left foot next to right	
	Vine Left	
13	Step left foot to left	⇦
14	Cross right foot behind left	

Beats	Movement	Direction
15	Step left foot to left	
16	Stomp right foot next to left	
	Charlestons	
17	Step right foot forward	
18	Kick left foot forward and clap	
19	Step left foot back	
20	Touch right toe back and clap	
21	Step right foot forward	
22	Kick left foot forward and clap	
23	Step left foot back	
24	Touch right toe back and clap	
	Harpoon Hips	
25	Step right foot next to left and bump hips to right	
26	Bump hips to left	
27	Bump hips to right	
28	Bump hips to left *(put weight on left foot)*	
	Jazz Box	
29	Cross right foot over left, making quarter turn to right	
30	Step back on left foot	
31	Step right foot to right	
32	Stomp left next to right *(with weight on left)*	

Begin again!

☆☆ Hillbilly Rock, Hillbilly Roll ☆☆

Sheila Vee, Carol Hick and Rob Fowler, UK — ***Four Wall***

Beats	Movement	Direction
	Cross Recover	
1	Cross right foot over left	❍
&	Lift left foot and replace it	
2	Step right foot in place	
3	Cross left foot over right	
&	Lift right foot and replace it	
4	Step left foot back in place	
	Chassé Right, Stomp	
5	Step right foot to right side	⇨
&	Step left foot beside right	
6	Step right foot to right side	
&	Step left foot beside right	
7	Step right foot to right side	
&	Stomp left foot in place	
8	Stomp right foot in place	
	Rock Forward and Back	
9	Rock forward onto left foot	❍
&	Step right foot in place	
10	Rock back onto left foot	
&	Step right foot in place	
11	Step feet together, left foot beside right	

Beats	Movement	Direction
&	Swivel both heels left	❍
12	Swivel both heels centre	

Beats	Movement	Direction
	Quarter Turn Left, Camel Walk	
&	Turn quarter turn left on ball of right foot	◖
13	Step left foot forward (2 lasso swings over head with right hand)	⇧
&	Slide right foot beside left	
14	Step left foot forward	
15	Slight pause, right foot in place	
&16	Place hand behind your head and bump hips forward twice	

32-STEP VARIATION BY
ÁINE QUINN

Beats	Movement	Direction
1–12	As steps 1–12 above	

Beats	Movement	Direction
13	Tap right heel forward	❍
&	Step right foot in place	
14	Tap left heel forward	
&	Step left foot in place	
15	Tap right heel forward	
&	Step right foot in place	
16	Tap left heel forward	
&	Step left foot in place	

(Contd.)

Beats	Movement	Direction
	Down, Up, Down, Up, Slap Leather	
17	Tap ball of right foot down	
&	Hitch right knee and slap thigh with right hand	
18	Tap ball of right foot down	
&	Hitch right knee and slap thigh with right hand	
19	Point right toe forward	
&	Point right toe to right side	
20	Swing right leg behind left, slap right heel with left hand	
&	Point right toe to right side	
21	Swing right leg in front of left, slap right heel with left hand	
&	Swing right leg out to right side, turning quarter turn left, slap right heel with right hand	
	Right Vine, Slap	
22	Step right foot to right side	
&	Step left foot behind right	
23	Step right foot to right side	
&	Swing left leg behind right, slap left heel with right hand	
	Left Vine, Slap	
24	Step left foot to left side	

Beats	Movement	Direction
&	Step right foot behind left	⇦
25	Step left foot to left side	
&	Swing right leg behind left, slap right heel with left hand	

Walk Backwards, Camel Walk Forward

Beats	Movement	Direction
26&27	Walk back, right, left, right	⇩
&	Hitch left knee	
28	Step left foot forward	
&	Slide right foot to meet left (2 lasso swings overhead with right hand)	
29	Step left foot forward	⇧
&	Slide right foot to meet left	
30	Swivel both heels left	
&	Swivel both heels centre	
31	Pause, place right hand behind head	○
&32	Bump hips forward twice	

Begin again!

☆☆☆☆☆☆☆ *Hog Wild* ☆☆☆☆☆☆☆

Robert C. Weaver, Crooksville, USA — ***Four Wall***

Beats	Movement	Direction
	Right Toe Touches	
1	Touch right toes forward	○
2	Touch right toes to right side	
3&4	Triple-step in place (right, left, right)	
	Left Toe Touches	
5	Touch left toes forward	○
6	Touch left toes to left side	
7&8	Triple-step in place (left, right, left)	
	Modified Grapevines	
9	Step right foot to right	⇨
10	Step left foot behind right	
11&12	Triple-step in place (right, left, right)	
13	Step left foot to left	⇦
14	Step right foot behind left	
15&16	Triple-step in place (left, right, left), making a quarter turn to left	◣
	Rock Steps with Half Turn	
17	Rock forward onto right foot	○
18	Step back onto left foot	

Beats	Movement	Direction
19&20	Make half turn to right while doing triple-step in place (right, left, right)	◗
21	Rock forward onto left foot	❍
22	Step back onto right foot	
23&24	Make half turn to left while doing triple-step in place (left, right, left)	◖
	Kicks	
25	Kick right foot forward	❍
26	Kick right foot to right side	
27&28	Triple-step in place (right, left, right)	
29	Kick left foot forward	
30	Kick left foot to left side	
31&32	Triple-step in place (left, right, left)	

Begin again!

☆☆☆☆☆ *Honky Tonkin'* ☆☆☆☆☆

Marlene and Bob Peyne-Ferry, Westville, USA — ***Four Wall***

Beats	Movement	Direction
	Right Vine	
1	Step right foot to right	⇨
2	Step left foot behind right	
3	Step right foot to right	
4	Scuff left foot forward	
	Left Vine	
5	Step left foot to left	⇦
6	Step right foot behind left	
7	Step left foot to left	
8	Scuff right foot forward	
	Stomp Forward	
9	Stomp right foot forward, switching weight to right	⇧
10	Hold and clap	
11	Stomp left foot forward, switching weight to left	
12	Hold and clap	
	Right Monterey Half Turn	
13	Touch right toe to right	○

Beats	Movement	Direction
14	Make half turn to right, stepping right next to left	
15	Touch left toe to left	
16	Step left foot next to right	
	Stomp Forward	
17	Stomp right foot forward, switching weight to right	
18	Hold and clap	
19	Stomp left foot forward, switching weight to left	
20	Hold and clap	
	Right Monterey Half Turn	
21	Touch right toe to right	
22	Make half turn to right, stepping right next to left	
23	Touch left toe to left	
24	Step left foot next to right	
	Jazz Box with Quarter Turn	
25	Step left foot over right	
26	Step right foot back, making quarter turn to left	
27	Step left foot to left of right foot	
28	Step right foot next to left	

(Contd.)

Beats	Movement	Direction
	Kick-Ball-Change	
29	Kick right foot forward	❍
&	Step on ball of right foot quickly	
30	Step left foot in place	
	Half Turn	
31	Step right foot forward	◖
32	Make half turn to left	

Begin again!

☆☆☆☆ Honky Tonk Stomp ☆☆☆☆

Two Wall

Beats	Movement	Direction
	Pigeon Toes	
1	Split heels out	❍
2	Heels in	
3	Split heels out	
4	Heels in	
	Doubles	
5,6	Tap right heel forward twice	❍
7,8	Tap right toe behind twice	
9	Tap right heel forward	❍
10	Feet together	
11,12	Stomp left foot twice	
13	Tap left heel forward	
14,	Feet together	
15,16	Stomp right foot twice	
	Vine Right	
17	Step right foot to right side	⇨
18	Cross left foot behind right	
19	Step right foot to right side	
20	Kick left foot across right leg and clap	

(Contd.)

Beats	Movement	Direction
	Vine Left with Half Turn	
21	Step left foot to left side	
22	Cross right foot behind left	
23	Step left foot to left side	
24	Swivel half turn to left, with weight on left leg	
25	Step right foot to right side	
26	Cross left foot behind right	
27	Step right foot to right side	
28	Kick left foot across right leg and clap	
	Vine Left	
29	Step left foot to left side	
30	Cross right foot behind left	
31	Step left foot to left side	
32	Stomp right foot beside left foot to finish	

Begin again!

☆☆☆☆ Honky Tonk Twist 2 ☆☆☆☆

(a.k.a. Twistin' the Night Away)

Max Perry, Danbury, USA — ***Four Wall***

Beats	Movement	Direction
	Twist Heels Right	
1	Twist both heels to right	❍
2	Bring heels back to centre	
3–4	Repeat steps 1–2	
5	Touch right heel forward	❍
6	Hook right foot in front of left	
7	Touch right heel forward	
8	Step right foot next to left	
	Twist Heels Left	
9	Twist both heels to left	❍
10	Bring heels back to centre	
11–12	Repeat steps 9–10	
13	Touch left heel forward	❍
14	Hook left foot in front of right	
15	Touch left heel forward	
16	Touch left toe next to right foot	
	Forward Scuff	
17	Step left foot forward	⇧
18	Scuff right foot forward	

(Contd.)

Beats	Movement	Direction
19	Step right foot forward	⇧
20	Scuff left foot forward	
	Walk Back	
21	Step left foot back	⇩
22	Step right foot back	
23	Step left foot back	
24	Step right foot next to left	
	Travelling Twists	
25	Twist both heels to left	⇦
26	Twist both toes to left	
27	Twist both heels to left	
28	Twist both toes to left	
29	Twist both toes to right	⇨
30	Twist both heels to right	
31	Twist both toes to right	
32	Twist both heels to centre, then shift weight to left foot	
	Monterey Turn	
33	Touch right toe to right side	
34	Make half turn to right *(swing right leg around)* and step right foot next to left	◗
35	Touch left toe to left side	
36	Step left foot next to right	

Beats	Movement	Direction
	Toe Struts Back	
37	Step back on ball of right foot	⇩
38	Lower right heel	
39	Step back on ball of left foot, next to right foot	
40	Lower left heel	
	Hand Jive	
41–42	Slap both hands on thighs twice	○
43–44	Clap hands twice at chest level	
45–46	Raise right arm in hitchhiking motion with thumb pointed back, twice	
47–48	Lower right arm and raise left arm in same hitchhiking motion, twice	
	Heel Struts Forward	
49	Step forward with right heel	⇧
50	Lower ball of right foot	
51	Step forward with left heel	
52	Lower ball of left foot	
	Step and Quarter Turn	
53	Step right foot forward	
54	Hold	
55	Make quarter turn to left, shifting weight to left foot	◾
56	Hold	

(Contd.)

Beats	Movement	Direction
	Jazz Box	
57	Cross right foot over left	❍
58	Step back on left foot	
59	Step right foot to right side	
60	Step left foot next to right	
61–64	Twist both heels to left, centre, left, centre	

Begin again!

☆☆☆☆ Hooked on Country ☆☆☆☆

Four Wall

Beats	Movement	Direction
	Right Shuffle Back	
1	Step right foot back	⇩
&	Step left foot back beside right	
2	Step right foot back	
	Left Shuffle Back	
3	Step left foot back	⇩
&	Step right foot back beside left	
4	Step left foot back	
	Walk Forward	
5	Step right foot forward	⇧
6	Step left foot forward	
7	Step right foot forward	
8	Kick left foot forward and clap	
	Walk Backward and Ball Change	
9	Step left foot back	⇩
10	Step right foot back	
11	Step left foot back	
&	Step on ball of right foot	
12	Cross left foot over right, taking weight on left	

(Contd.)

Beats	Movement	Direction
	Vine Right	
13	Step right foot to right side	⇨
14	Step left foot behind right	
15	Step right foot to right side	
16	Kick left foot across right and clap	
	Vine Left	
17	Step left foot to left side	⇦
18	Step right foot behind left	
19	Step left foot to left side	
20	Kick right foot across left and clap	
	Step and Kick	
21	Step right foot in place	○
22	Kick left foot across and clap	
23	Step left foot in place	
24	Kick right foot across and clap	
	Taps	
25,26	Tap right heel forward, twice	○
27,28	Tap right toe behind, twice	
	Heel Turn	
29	Tap right heel forward	
30	Quarter turn to left	◖
31	Stomp right foot	
32	Kick right foot	
	Begin again!	

☆☆☆☆☆☆ Norma Jean ☆☆☆☆☆☆

Donna and Dena Wasnick, Tulare, USA **_Four Wall_**

Beats	Movement	Direction
	Toe-Heel-Clap-Step	
1	Touch right toe forward	⇧
2	Step right heel down	
3	Touch left toe forward	
4	Step left heel down	
5	Touch right toe forward	
6	Hold and clap	
7	Step right heel down	
8	Step left next to right	
	Repeat	
9	Touch right toe forward	⇧
10	Step right heel down	
11	Touch left toe forward	
12	Step left heel down	
13	Touch right toe forward	
14	Hold and clap	
15	Step right heel down	
16	Step left next to right	
	Step Touches	
17	Step back on right foot	

(Contd.)

Beats	Movement	Direction
18	Touch left foot next to right	◑
19	Step left foot to left side	
20	Touch right foot next to left	
21	Step right foot to right side, making quarter turn to right	◗
22	Touch let foot next to right	
23	Step left foot to left side	
24	Touch right foot next to left	

Scoot-Fan-Stomp

Beats	Movement	Direction
25	Scoot on left foot while raising right knee	⇧
26	Touch right toe down next to left	
27	Scoot on left foot while raising right knee	
28	Step down on right foot	
29	Fan both heels out	◑
30	Fan both heels in	
31	Stomp right foot *(don't put weight on it)*	
32	Stomp right foot *(don't put weight on it)*	

Begin again!

☆☆☆☆☆ Out with a Bang ☆☆☆☆☆

Max Perry, Danbury, USA **Four Wall**

The '&' symbol stands for a half count. For example, in steps &1 you need to make two moves in one count of music.

Beats	Movement	Direction
	Jazz Jump Forward	
&	Jump forward, right foot down first,	⇧
1	then left foot down	
2	Clap	
	Jazz Jump Back	
&	Jump back, right foot down first,	⇩
3	then left foot down	
4	Clap	
5	Step forward on right foot	⇧
6	Scuff left foot	
7	Step forward on left foot	
8	Scuff right foot	
	Rock Steps	
9	Rock forward on right foot	○
10	Step left foot in place	
11	Rock back on right foot	
12	Step left foot in place	

(Contd.)

Beats	Movement	Direction
	Unwinding Turn	
13	Cross right foot over left	
14	Unwind, making half turn to left *(weight on balls of both feet)*	◖
	Out and In	
&	Small side step to right on right foot	❍
15	Small side step to left on left foot	
&	Small step to centre with right foot	
16	Step left foot next to right	
17	Step forward on right foot	⇧
18	Hitch left leg	
19	Step forward on left foot	
20	Hitch right leg	
21	Step forward on right foot	
22	Hitch left leg	
23	Step forward on left foot	
24	Hitch right leg	
	Right Vine	
25	Step right foot to right	⇨
26	Step left foot behind right	
27	Step right foot to right	
28	Scuff left foot	

Beats	Movement	Direction
	Left Vine with Turn	
29	Step left foot to left	⇦
30	Step right foot behind left	
31	Step left foot to left, making quarter turn to left	◖
32	Scuff right foot	

Begin again!

☆☆☆☆ Redneck Macarena ☆☆☆☆

Two Wall

Beats	Movement	Direction
	Arm Movements	
1	Right arm out horizontally in front, palm facing down	❍
2	Left arm out horizontally in front, palm facing down	
3	Right arm, same position, turn palm up	❍
4	Left arm, same position, turn palm up	
5	Right hand, touch left shoulder	❍
6	Left hand, touch right shoulder	
7	Right hand, touch behind the head	❍
8	Left hand, touch behind the head	
9	Right hand, across body, touch left hip	❍
10	Left hand, across body, touch right hip	
11	Right hand, behind body, touch right buttock	❍
12	Left hand, behind body, touch left buttock	

Beats	Movement	Direction
13–15	Hands on buttocks, bend knees, rotate hips anticlockwise turning quarter turn left	○
16	Jump feet together, clap	
	Triple-steps, Right and Left	
17	Step right foot quarter turn right	◔
&	Step left foot beside right	
18	Step right foot beside left	
19	Step left foot half turn left	◖
&	Step right foot beside left	
20	Step left foot beside right	
	Step and Hitch	
21	Step right foot forward making quarter turn to right to face original wall	◔
22	Touch left foot beside right	
23	Step left foot back	
24	Touch right foot beside left	
	Heel Digs	
25	Tap right heel forward	○
26	Step right foot in place	
27	Tap left heel forward	
28	Step left foot in place	

(Contd.)

Beats	Movement	Direction
29	***Mexican Heels***	❍
&	Tap right heel forward	❍
	Step on ball of right foot	
	(to switch heels)	
30	Tap left heel forward	
&	Step on ball of left foot	
31&	Repeat Mexican Heels, turning half	◖
32	turn left	
	Begin again!	

☆☆☆☆☆ Reggae Cowboy ☆☆☆☆☆

Gene Schrivener, San Juan Capistrano, USA **Four Wall**

The tricky part is the shuffle-steps, which are executed at 45° angles except for the last one when you directly face a new wall. Pay attention to the direction and angle of the shuffle-steps and the rest is a snap! The '&' symbol represents an extra beat.

Beats	Movement	Direction
1	Step with right foot	⇧
2	Lift left knee and clap	
3	Step with left foot	
4	Lift right knee and clap	
5	Step with right foot	
6	Lift left knee and clap	
7	Step with left foot	
8	Lift right knee and clap	
9	Step back on right	⇩
10	Step back on left	
11	Step back on right	
12	Lift left knee and clap	
13	Step back on left	
14	Step back on right	
15	Step back on left	
16	Lift right knee and clap	

(Contd.)

Beats	Movement	Direction
	Vine Right	
17	Step to right with right foot	⇨
18	Step behind right with left foot	
19	Step to right with right foot	
20	Scuff left foot next to right	
	Vine Left	
21	Step to left with left foot	⇦
22	Step behind left with right foot	
23	Step to left with left foot	
24	Scuff right foot next to left	
	Vine Right	
25	Step to right with right foot	⇨
26	Step behind right with left foot	
27	Step to right with right foot	
28	Scuff left foot next to right	
	Vine Left	
29	Step to left with left foot	⇦
30	Step behind left with right foot	
31	Step to left with left foot	
32	Scuff right foot next to left	
	Turn 1/8 Turn to Right *(1.30 o'clock)*	
33&34	Right shuffle-step forward (right, left, right)	⬀

Beats	Movement	Direction
35&36	Left shuffle-step forward (left, right, left)	⇗
	Turn Quarter Turn to Right *(4.30 o'clock)*	◗
37&38	Right shuffle-step backward	⇘
39&40	Left shuffle-step backward	
	Turn Quarter Turn to Right *(7.30 o'clock)*	◗
41&42	Right shuffle-step forward	⇗
43&44	Left shuffle-step forward	
	Turn 1/8 Turn to Right *(9 o'clock)* *(You are now facing the wall to the left of*	
45&46	*the original wall you were facing)*	
47&48	Right shuffle-step backward	⇩
	Left shuffle-step backward	

Begin again!

☆☆☆☆☆ Rockin' the House ☆☆☆☆☆

Max Perry, Danbury, USA **Four Wall**

If using If the House is Rockin' *by Lee Roy Parnell, wait until Lee Roy says, 'I'm glad you called,' count 6, 7, 8, then begin. The dance actually starts on the phrase 'We got a party goin' on'.*

Beats	Movement	Direction
1	Tap right toes in, next to left foot	
2	Tap right heel out to side, with toes pointing out	
3	Step right foot in front and slightly to left of left foot	⇧
4	Clap	
5	Tap left toes in, next to right foot	
6	Tap left heel out to side, with toes pointing out	
7	Step left foot in front and slightly to right of right foot	⇧
8	Clap	
9	Kick right foot forward	
10	Step right foot back and cross behind left	⇩
11	Kick left foot out	
12	Step left foot back and cross behind right	

Beats	Movement	Direction
13	Kick right foot forward	
14	Step right foot back and cross behind left	⇩
15	Kick left foot out	
16	Step left foot back and cross behind right	
17&18	Shuffle-step forward (right, left, right)	⇧
19&20	Shuffle-step forward (left, right, left)	
21	Step forward on right foot	
22	Make half turn to left	◖
23	Step forward on right foot	
24	Make half turn to left	◖
	Step Slides	
25	Step right foot to right side	⇨
26–28	Slow-slide left foot next to right, arms out to side	
29	Big-step left foot to left side	⇦
30–32	Slow-slide right foot next to left, arms out to side	
	Walk Back	
33	Step right foot back	⇩
34	Step left foot back	
35	Step right foot back	

(Contd.)

Beats	Movement	Direction
36	Touch left foot next to right	❍
37	Step left foot forward	⇧
38	Step right foot forward, making quarter turn to left	
39	Step left foot next to right	
40	Stomp right foot in place	
	Foot Boogies	
41	Turn left toes out	❍
42	Turn left heel out	
43	Turn left heel in	
44	Turn left toes in to centre	

Begin again!

☆☆☆☆☆☆ Rocky Top ☆☆☆☆☆☆

Two Wall

Beats	Movement	Direction
	Toe Touches, Walking Steps, Swivels	
1	Touch right toe out to right side	❍
2	Touch right toe directly back	
3	Touch right toe out to right side	
4	Cross right foot over left *(taking weight)*	
5,6	Step left foot back. Step right foot back	
7,8	Step left foot forward. Step right foot beside left	
	Travelling to right . . .	
9–12	Swivel heels right, toes right, heels right, toes right	⇨
	Repeat steps 1–12 with left foot leading . . .	
13	Touch left toe out to left side	❍
14	Touch left toe directly back	
15	Touch left toe out to left side	
16	Cross left foot over right *(taking weight)*	
17,18	Step right foot back. Step left foot back	

(Contd.)

Beats	Movement	Direction
19,20	Step right foot forward. Step left foot beside right	
21–24	Swivel heels left, toes left, heels left, toes left	⇦
	Walk Backwards, Chug, Rock, Turn	
25,26	Step right foot back. Step left foot back	⇩
27,28	Step right foot back. Chug on right foot *(hitch left knee and hop on right foot)*	
29	Rock forward onto left foot	○
30	Rock back onto right foot	
31	Rock forward onto left foot	
32	Pivot quarter turn left, stepping right foot beside left	◢
	Toe Touches	
33	Touch right foot out to right side	○
34	Step right foot beside left	
35	Touch left toe out to left side	
36	Step left foot beside right	
37–40	Repeat steps 33–36	
	Heel, Toe, Turn, Stomp	
41	Tap right heel forward	○
42	Touch right toe back	

Beats	Movement	Direction
43,44	Repeat steps 41,42	
45	Turn quarter turn left, stepping on right foot	◀
46	Stomp left foot in place	
47,48	Stomp right foot beside left twice	

Begin again!

☆ Ski-Bumpus (a.k.a. Black Velvet) ☆

Linda Deford, Knoxville, USA — **One Wall**

This line dance may be danced in opposing lines.

Beats	Movement	Direction
	Right and Left Shuffle, Pivot Turn	
1	Step right foot forward	⇧
&	Step left foot beside right	
2	Step right foot forward	
3	Step left foot forward	
&	Step right foot beside left	
4	Step left foot forward	
5	Step right foot forward	
6	Pivot half turn left	◖
7–12	Repeat steps 1–6	⇧
	Jazz Box	
13	Cross right foot over left	○
14	Step left foot back	
15	Step right foot to right side	
16	Step left foot beside right	
17–20	Repeat steps 13–16	○
	Side Touches	
21	Touch right toe out to right side	○

Beats	Movement	Direction
22	Step right foot beside left	
23	Touch left toe out to left side	
24	Step left foot beside right	
25–28	Repeat steps 21–24	
	Right Kick-Ball-Change and Pivot Turn	
29	Kick right foot forward	
&	Step on ball of right foot	
30	Step left foot beside right	
31&32	Repeat steps 29&30	
33	Step right foot forward	
34	Pivot half turn left	
35–40	Repeat steps 29–34	
	Begin again!	

☆☆☆☆ South-Side Shuffle ☆☆☆☆

Two Wall

Beats	Movement	Direction
	Toe Fans	
1	Fan right toe out	❍
2	Fan right toe in	
3	Fan right toe out	
4	Fan right toe in	
	Doubles	
5,6	Tap right heel forward twice	❍
7,8	Tap right toe behind twice	
	Singles	
9	Tap right heel forward	❍
10	Tap right toe behind	
11	Tap right toe to right side	
12	Tap right toe behind left	
	Vine Right	
13	Step right foot to right side	⇨
14	Cross left foot behind right	
15	Step right foot to right side	
16	Scoop left foot forward	

Beats	Movement	Direction
	Vine Left	
17	Step left foot to left side	⇦
18	Cross right foot behind left	
19	Step left foot to left side	
20	Scoop right foot forward	
21	Step right foot forward	⇧
22	Slide left foot to meet right	
23	Step right foot forward	
24	Pivot half turn right *(with weight on right leg)*	◗
25	Step left foot back	⇩
26	Slide right foot back to meet left	
27	Step left foot back	
28	Stomp right foot beside left	

Begin again!

☆☆☆☆☆☆☆ Star Kick ☆☆☆☆☆☆☆

Two Wall

Beats	Movement	Direction
	Left and Right Shuffles Forward	
1	Step left foot forward	⇧
&	Step right foot beside left	
2	Step left foot forward	
3	Step right foot forward	
&	Step left foot beside right	
4	Step right foot forward	
	Walk Back and Ball Change	
5	Step left foot back	⇩
6	Step right foot back	
7	Step left foot back	
&	Step on ball of right foot	
8	Cross left foot over right	
	Right Vine and Scuff Kick	
9	Step right foot to right side	⇨
10	Step left foot behind right	
11	Step right foot to right side	
12	Scuff left foot forward ending with a hitch (raise left knee)	

Beats	Movement	Direction
	Left Vine and Scuff Kick	
13	Step left foot to left side	⇦
14	Step right foot behind left	
15	Step left foot to left side	
16	Scuff right foot forward ending with a hitch (raise right knee)	
	Right and Left Shuffle Forward and Pivot Turn	
17	Step right foot forward	⇧
&	Step left foot beside right	
18	Step right foot forward	
19	Step left foot forward	
&	Step right foot forward	
20	Step left foot forward	
21	Step right foot forward	
22	Pivot half turn left	◖
	Right Shuffle Forward and Pivot Twice	
23	Step right foot forward	⇧
&	Step left foot beside right	
24	Step right foot forward	
25	Step left foot forward	
26	Pivot half turn right	◗
27,28	Repeat steps 25,26	

(Contd.)

Beats	Movement	Direction
	Hip Sways	
29	Step left foot forward, sway hips forward	❍
30	Sway hips back	
31	Sway hips forward	
32	Sway hips back ending with weight on right foot	

Begin again!

☆☆☆☆☆ Swing City Jive ☆☆☆☆☆

Hillbilly Rick and Linda Mosby, Haubstadt, USA **Four Wall**

Beats	Movement	Direction
	Rock Forward and Back	
1	Rock right foot forward	❍
2	Rock left foot in place	
3	Rock back onto right foot	
4	Rock left foot in place	
5,6	Repeat steps 1,2	
7,8	Step right foot beside left, hold	
	Side Touches, Cross, Side, Together, Hold	
9,10	Touch left toe to left side, hold	❍
11,12	Touch left toe beside right, hold	
13	Touch left toe to left side	
14	Touch left toe beside right	
15,16	Touch left toe to left side, hold	
17	Cross left foot behind right	⇨
18	Step right foot to right side	
19,20	Step left foot beside right, hold	
	Repeat Steps 9–20 leading with right foot . . .	
21,22	Touch right toe to right side, hold	❍
23,24	Touch right toe beside left, hold	

(Contd.)

Beats	Movement	Direction
25	Touch right toe to right side	❍
26	Touch right toe beside left	
27,28	Touch right toe to right side, hold	
29	Cross right foot behind left	⇦
30	Step left foot to left side	
31,32	Step right foot beside left, hold	
	Rock Forward and Back	
33	Rock left foot forward	❍
34	Rock right foot in place	
35	Rock back onto left foot	
36	Rock right foot in place	
37,38	Repeat steps 33, 34	
39,40	Step left foot beside right, hold	
	Stomp Forward	
41,42	Stomp right foot forward, hold	⇧
43,44	Stomp left foot forward, hold	
45	Stomp right foot forward across left	
46	Stomp left foot forward across right	
47,48	Stomp right foot forward and left, hold	
	Pivot Half Turn Right, Quarter Turn Left	
49,50	Step left foot forward, hold	
51,52	Pivot half turn right, hold	◗

Beats	Movement	Direction
53	Step left foot forward	
54	Slide right foot behind left	
55	Step left foot forward turning quarter turn left	
56	Scuff right foot forward	

Jazz Box, Heel and Toe Splits

Beats	Movement	Direction
57	Cross right foot over left	
58	Step left foot back	
59	Step right foot to right side	
60	Step left foot beside right	
61,62	Split heels out, in	
63,64	Split toes out, in	

Begin again!

☆☆☆☆ Symphony Shuffle ☆☆☆☆

Esther D'Arpino, Conklin, USA — ***Two Wall***

Beats	Movement	Direction
	Vine Right	
1	Step right foot to right	⇨
2	Step left foot behind right	
3	Step right foot to right	
4	Kick left foot	
	Vine Left	
5	Step left foot to left	⇦
6	Step right foot behind left	
7	Step left foot to left	
8	Kick right foot	
	Forward Walk	
9	Right step forward	⇧
10	Left step forward	
11	Right step forward	
12	Left step forward	
	Jazz Box	
13	Step right foot over left	❍
14	Step back on left foot	
15	Step back on right *(to the right of left)*	
16	Step left foot next to right	

Beats	Movement	Direction
	Right Shuffle-step	
17	Step right foot forward	⇧
&	Slide left foot up to right	
18	Slide right foot forward	
	Left Shuffle-step	
19	Step left foot forward	⇧
&	Slide right foot up to left	
20	Slide left foot forward	
	Half Turn to Left	
21	Step right foot forward	
22	Make half turn to left (*shifting weight to left foot)*	◖
	Stomps	
23	Stomp right foot next to left, shift weight to right foot	○
24	Stomp left foot next to right, shift weight to left foot	
	Begin again!	

☆☆☆☆☆☆ The Tall T ☆☆☆☆☆☆

Thom E. Branton, Moncks Corner, USA ***Four Wall***

Beats	Movement	Direction
	Right Hook	
1	Tap right heel forward	❍
2	Cross right foot over left shin	
3	Tap right heel forward	
4	Step right foot next to left	
	Twist	
5	Swivel both heels to right . . .	❍
6	to left . . .	
7	to right . . .	
8	to centre	
	Left Hook	
9	Tap left heel forward	❍
10	Cross left foot over right shin	
11	Tap left heel forward	
12	Step left foot next to right	
	Twist	
13	Swivel both heels to left . . .	❍
14	to right . . .	
15	to left . . .	
16	to centre	

Beats	Movement	Direction
	Heel Taps	
17–18	Tap right heel forward twice	❍
	Back Toe Taps	
19–20	Tap right toe back twice	❍
	Toe Points	
21	Point right toe to right	❍
22	Step right foot next to left	
23	Point left toe to left	
24	Step left foot next to right	
	Vine Right	
25	Step right foot to right	⇨
26	Cross left foot behind right	
27	Step right foot to right	
28	Brush left foot forward	
	Vine Left with Quarter Turn	
29	Step left foot to left	⇦
30	Cross right foot behind left	
31	Step left foot to left, making quarter turn to left	◾
32	Brush right foot forward	

Begin again!

☆☆☆☆☆☆ *Texas Twist* ☆☆☆☆☆☆

Four Wall

Beats	Movement	Direction
1	Swivel both heels right	❍
2	Swivel both heels to centre	
3–8	Repeat steps 1 & 2, (three times)	
9	Tap right heel forward	❍
10	Touch right foot beside left	
11	Step right foot to right side	
12	Swivel quarter turn to left *(changing weight to left)*	◖
13	Touch right toes to right side	❍
14	Hitch right knee close to left	
15	Touch right toes to right side	
16	Hitch right knee close to left	
	Right Vine	
17	Step right foot to right side	⇨
18	Step left foot behind right	
19	Step right foot to right side	
20	Touch left foot beside right	❍
21	Touch left toes to left side	
22	Hitch left knee close to right	
23	Touch left toes to left side	
24	Hitch left knee close to right	

Beats	Movement	Direction
	Left Vine	
25	Step left foot to left side	⇦
26	Step right foot behind left	
27	Step left foot to left side	
28	Step right foot beside left	

Begin again!

☆☆☆☆☆ Trashy Women ☆☆☆☆☆

Four Wall

Beats	Movement	Direction
	Heel Taps	
1	Tap left heel forward 45 degrees left	❍
2	Step left foot back in place	
3	Tap right heel forward 45 degrees right	
4	Step right foot back in place	
5,6	Touch left heel forward 45 degrees left, tap twice	
7,8	Cross left foot over right in front, tap heel twice	
9	Tap left heel out to left side	
10	Cross left foot over right and tap heel once	
11,12	Repeat steps 9,10	
	Switch Feet, Thrust Hips	
&	Jump left foot back	❍
13	Extend right foot forward	
14–16	Thrust hips forward twice *(Draw fisted arms back as hips go forward)*	
	Right Vine	
17	Step right foot to right side turning quarter turn left to face 9 o'clock	◖

Beats	Movement	Direction
18	Step left foot behind right	⇨
19	Step right foot to right side	
20	Scuff left foot forward	
	Left Vine	
21	Step left foot to left side	⇦
22	Step right foot behind left	
23	Step left foot to left side	
24	Scuff right foot forward	
	Walk Backwards	
25	Step right foot back	⇩
26	Step left foot back	
27	Step right foot back	
28	Scuff left foot forward	
	Step and Slide Forward	
29	Step left foot forward	⇧
30	Slide right foot up to meet left	
31	Step left foot forward	
32	Stomp right foot beside left	

Begin again!

☆☆☆☆☆☆ Tulsa Time ☆☆☆☆☆☆

Four Wall

Cha-Cha is a triple-step, making 3 steps in two beats. This dance will suit any Cha-Cha song.

Beats	Movement	Direction
	Rock Steps	
1	Rock forward on right foot	❍
2	Rock back on left foot	
3&4	Cha-Cha in place . . . right, left, right	
5	Rock back on left foot	❍
6	Rock forward on right foot	
7&8	Cha-Cha in place . . . left, right, left	
	Sailor-steps Forward	
9	Swing right foot forward, crossing over left	⇧
10	Swing left foot forward, crossing over right	
11&12	Cha-Cha in place . . . right, left, right	❍
13	Swing left foot forward, crossing over right	⇧
14	Swing right foot forward, crossing over left	
15&16	Cha-Cha in place . . . left, right, left	❍

Beats	Movement	Direction
17–24	Repeat steps 1–8	
	Modified Right Vine	
25	Step right foot to right side	
26	Step left foot behind right	
27&28	Cha-Cha in place . . . right, left, right	
	Modified Left Vine with Quarter Turn	
29	Step left foot to left side	
30	Step right foot behind left	
31&32	Cha-Cha . . . left, right, left, turning quarter to left	
	Begin again!	

☆☆☆☆☆☆ Twelve Step ☆☆☆☆☆☆

Four Wall

Beats	Movement	Direction
	Heel Digs, Swings and Hook	
1	Tap left heel forward	❍
2	Step left foot in place	
3	Tap right heel forward	
4	Step right foot in place	
5	Tap left heel forward	
6	Step left foot in place	
7,8	Tap right heel forward twice	
9,10	Tap right toe behind twice	
11	Tap right heel forward	
12	Tap left toe behind	
13	Swing right foot directly forward	
14	Swing right foot directly back	
15	Swing right foot directly forward	
16	Hook right foot across left shin, turning quarter turn left on left foot	◖
	Right Vine	
17	Step right foot to right side	⇨
18	Step left foot behind right	
19	Step right foot to right side	
20	Tap left foot beside right	

Beats	Movement	Direction
	Left Vine	
21	Step left foot to left side	⇦
22	Step right foot behind right	
23	Step left foot to left side	
24	Tap right foot beside left	
	Walk Back	
25	Step right foot back	⇩
26	Step left foot back	
27	Step right foot back	
28	Tap left foot beside right	
	Drag Steps	
29	Step left foot forward	⇧
30	Slide right foot to meet left	
31	Step left foot forward	
32	Slide right foot to meet left	
	Heel Swivels	
33	Swivel heels right	○
34	Swivel heels left	
35	Swivel heels right	
36	Swivel heels centre	

Begin again!

☆☆☆☆☆☆ Valley Rock ☆☆☆☆☆☆

Hank and Mary Dahl, Louisville, USA — ***Four Wall***

Beats	Movement	Direction
	Kick-Ball-Change	
1	Kick right foot forward	❍
&	Step ball of right foot next to left	
2	Step left foot in place	
3	Kick right foot forward	
&	Step ball of right foot next to left	
4	Step left foot in place	
	Right Heel Hook	
5	Touch right heel forward	❍
6	Hook right heel in front of left knee *(or shin)*	
7	Touch right heel forward	
8	Step right foot next to left	
	Kick-Ball-Change	
9	Kick left foot forward	❍
&	Step ball of left foot next to right	
10	Step right foot in place	
11	Kick left foot forward	
&	Step ball of left foot next to right	
12	Step right foot in place	

Beats	Movement	Direction
	Left Heel Hook	
13	Touch left heel forward	❍
14	Hook left foot in front of right knee *(or shin)*	
15	Touch left heel forward	
16	Step left foot next to right	
	Skate Slide Right	
17	Slide right foot to right side	⇨
18	Slide left foot next to right	
19	Slide right foot to right side	
20	Touch left foot next to right	
	Rolling Turn Left	
21	Starting half turn to left, step left foot to left side	⇦
22	Finishing half turn to left, step right foot past left	
23	Making half turn to left, step left foot to left side	
24	Touch right foot next to left	
25	Step right foot to right side	❍
26	Dig left toe beside right foot *(no weight change)*	
27	Step right foot to right side	
28	Dig left toe beside right foot *(no weight change)*	

(Contd.)

Beats	Movement	Direction
	Shuffle Right	
29	Making quarter turn to right, step right foot in place	◗
&	Step left foot in place	
30	Step right foot in place	
	Shuffle Left	
31	Making half turn to left, step left foot in place	◖
&	Step right foot in place	
32	Step left foot in place	

Begin again!

☆☆☆ The Watermelon Crawl ☆☆☆

Sue Lipscombe, Chicago, USA **Four Wall**

To dance the 'Watermelon Crawl' in opposing lines, line up facing each other. Miss out the quarter turn in step 23, so you'll keep facing the same direction. During the charlestons (steps 9–16) and slides (25–32), the lines will mix. Slap each others' hands!

Beats	Movement	Direction
	Sugarfoots	
1	Touch right toe beside left toe *(right knee is slightly bent and pointing inward, heel is raised)*	❍
2	Touch right heel beside left toe *(right toe and knee are pointing out)*	
3	Step right foot next to left	
&	Step left foot next to right *(in place)*	
4	Step right foot next to left *(in place)*	
5	Touch left toe beside right toe *(left knee is slightly bent and pointing inward, heel is raised)*	❍
6	Touch left heel beside right toe *(left toe and knee are pointing out)*	
7	Step left foot next to right	

(Contd.)

Beats	Movement	Direction
&	Step right foot next to left *(in place)*	❍
8	Step left foot next to right *(in place)*	
	Charlestons	
9	Step right foot forward	❍
10	Kick left foot forward and clap	
11	Step left foot back	
12	Touch right toe back and clap	
13	Step right foot forward	
14	Kick left foot forward and clap	
15	Step left foot back	
16	Touch right toe back and clap	
	Right Vine	
17	Step right foot to right side	⇨
18	Cross left foot behind right foot	
19	Step right foot to right side	
20	Kick left foot at forward diagonal	
	Left Vine with a Turn	
21	Step left foot to left side	⇦
22	Cross right foot behind left foot	
23	Step left foot to left side into a quarter turn to the left	◢
24	Touch right foot beside left and clap	

Beats	Movement	Direction
	Slides	
25	Take a long step forward with right foot, bending knees slightly	⇧
26	Slide left foot forward toward right foot *(don't stop motion)*	
27	Continue sliding left foot until it is beside right foot and stand up straight	
28	Clap	
29	Take a long step backward with left foot, bending knees slightly	⇩
30	Slide right foot back toward left foot *(don't stop motion)*	
31	Continue sliding right foot until it is beside left foot and stand up straight	
32	Clap	
	Heel Raises	
33	With weight on right foot, raise left heel and bump right hip to right side	○
34	Raise right heel and bump left hip to left side	
35	Raise left heel and bump right hip to right side	
36	Raise right heel and bump left hip to left side	

(Contd.)

Beats	Movement	Direction
	Pivot Turns	
37	Touch right foot forward	
38	Make half turn to left, taking the weight on the left foot	◖
39	Touch right foot forward	
40	Make half turn to left, taking the weight on the left foot	◖

Begin again!

☆☆☆☆ The Wrangler Wrap ☆☆☆☆

Max Perry, Danbury, USA ***Dance type***

Beats	Movement	Direction
	Rock and Shuffle	
1	Rock forward on left foot	○
2	Rock back on right foot	
3&4	Shuffle-step back (left, right, left)	⇩
5	Rock back on right foot	○
6	Rock forward on left foot	
7&8	Shuffle-step forward (right, left, right)	⇧
	Half Turns	
9	Step forward with left foot	●
10	Make half turn to right, shifting weight to right foot	
11	Step forward with left foot	
12	Make half turn to right, keep weight on left foot and hitch right knee. *(Another option: rock forward left, back on right, forward left, hitch right knee)*	
	Hip Bumps	
13	Step down with right foot, making quarter turn to right, bump hips right	◗
14	Bump hips left	

(Contd.)

Beats	Movement	Direction
15	Bump hips right	❍
16	Bump hips left	
	Rock and Shuffle	
17	Rock forward onto right foot across left	❍
18	Rock back on left	
19&20	Shuffle-step (right, left, right)	
21	Rock forward onto left foot across right	❍
22	Rock back on right	
23&24	Shuffle-step (left, right, left)	
	Big Turn	
25	Step right foot over left	❍
26	Make 360-degree turn with weight on left foot	
27&28	Shuffle-step forward (right, left, right)	⇧
	Walk Forward	
29	Step left	⇧
30	Step right	
31	Step left	
32	Make half turn to right, shifting weight to right foot	◗

Begin again!

Intermediate Level Dances

☆☆☆☆☆

☆☆☆☆☆☆ All Aboard ☆☆☆☆☆☆

Max Perry, Danbury and Jo Thompson, Nashville **Four Wall**

Beats	Movement	Direction
	Rock Steps and Coaster Step	
1	Rock forward onto right heel	❍
2	Step left foot in place	
3	Rock back onto right foot	
4	Step left foot in place	
5	Rock forward onto right heel	
6	Step left foot in place	
7	Step right foot back	
&	Step left foot beside right	
8	Step right foot forward	
	Repeat steps 1–8, left foot leading . . .	
9	Rock forward onto left heel	❍
10	Step right foot in place	
11	Rock back onto left foot	
12	Step right foot in place	
13	Rock forward onto left heel	
14	Step right foot in place	
15	Step left foot back	
&	Step right foot beside left	
16	Step left foot forward	
	Cross Ball Changes (travelling left)	
17	Cross right foot over left	

Beats	Movement	Direction
&	Step left foot to left side on ball of foot	⇦
18&	Repeat steps 17&	
19&	Repeat steps 17&	
20	Cross right foot over left	

Beats	Movement	Direction
	Syncopated Weave Right with Quarter Turn Right	
21	Cross left foot over right	⇨
22	Step right foot to right side	
23	Cross left behind right	
&	Step right forward, quarter turn right	◗
24	Step left foot forward	

Beats	Movement	Direction
	Pivot Turns Left	
25	Step right foot forward	●
26	Pivot half turn left	
27,28	Repeat steps 25,26	

Beats	Movement	Direction
	Chug Forward or Walk Forward	
29	Slide right foot forward on floor Raise left heel to pop left knee	⇧
30	Slide right foot forward, raising right heel to pop right knee, straighten left leg taking weight on left	
31,32	Repeat 29,30 *or* Walk forward right, left, right, left	

Begin again!

☆☆☆☆☆☆ All Shook Up ☆☆☆☆☆☆

Naomi Fleetwood, Columbus, USA — ***One Wall***

This is a 3-part dance, and its sequence is AB, ABC, ABC.

Beats	Movement	Direction
	PART A (32 counts)	
1&2	Shuffle forward, left, right, left	⇧
3&4	Shuffle forward right, left, right	
5,6	Left foot to left side. Right foot behind left	⇦
7,8	Left foot to left side. Touch right foot beside left	
	Shuffle Backwards, Right Vine with Touch	
9&10	Shuffle back, right, left, right	⇩
11&12	Shuffle back, left, right, left	
13,14	Right foot to right side. Left foot behind right	⇨
15,16	Right foot to right side. Touch left foot beside right	
	Walk Forward, Kick, Walk Backwards, Touch	
17–19	Walk forward, left, right, left	⇧

Beats	Movement	Direction
20	Kick right foot forward	
21–23	Walk back, right, left, right	⇩
24	Touch left foot beside right	
	'Elvis Knees'	
25,26	Extend left arm to left. Clap	❍
27,28	Extend left arm to left again, right hand on stomach. Hold	
29	Thrust hips to left, bend right knee over left knee	
30	Thrust hips to right, bend left knee over right knee	
31,32	Repeat steps 29,30	
	PART B (16 counts)	
	Left Vine, Pivot Turns, Right Vine, Pivot Turns	
1,2	Left foot to left side. Right behind left	⇦
3,4	Left foot to left side. Touch right foot beside left	
5,6	Step right foot forward. Pivot half turn left	◖
7,8	Repeat steps 5,6	
9,10	Right foot to right side. Left foot behind right	⇨
11,12	Right foot to right side. Touch left foot beside right	

(Contd.)

Beats	Movement	Direction
13,14	Step left foot forward. Pivot half turn right	◗
15,16	Repeat steps 13,14	

PART C (32 counts)

Left Vine with Turn, Walk Backwards, Touch, Strut Forward

Beats	Movement	Direction
1,2	Left foot to left side. Right foot behind left	⇦
3	Left foot to left side, turning quarter turn left	◖
4	Hitch right knee, turning quarter turn left	◖
5–7	Walk back, right, left, right	⇩
8	Touch left foot beside right	
9	Step left foot forward on ball of foot	⇧
10	Lower left heel to floor	
11	Step right foot forward on ball of	
12	foot	
13–16	Lower right heel to floor	
17–32	Repeat steps 9–12	
	Repeat steps 1–16	

☆☆☆☆☆☆ American Pie ☆☆☆☆☆☆

Chris Hodgson, c/o Wild Bills, UK — ***Four Wall***

Beats	Movement	Direction
	(16-beat introduction)	
	Right and Left Shuffles, Half Turn, Quarter Turn	
1&2	Shuffle forward, right, left, right	⇧
3&4	Shuffle forward, left, right, left	
5,6	Step right foot forward.	
	Pivot half turn left	◖
7,8	Step right foot forward.	
	Pivot quarter turn left	◢
	Stroll Forward, Kick, Stroll Back	
9,10	Step right foot forward.	⇧
	Step left foot forward	
11,12	Step right foot forward.	
	Kick left foot forward. Clap	
13,14	Step left foot back. Step right foot back	⇩
15,16	Step left foot back. Step right beside left	
	Jump, Cross, Unwind, Clap	
17	Jump feet shoulder width apart	○
18	Jump crossing right foot over left	
19,20	Unwind half turn left. Clap	◖
21–24	Repeat steps 17–20	

(Contd.)

Beats	Movement	Direction
	Syncopated Weave Right	
25,26	Step right foot to right side. Step left foot behind right	⇨
&27	Step right foot to right side. Cross left foot over right	
28	Touch right toe to right side	
	Scoots and Monterey Turn	
29,30	Step right foot in place. Hitch left knee, scoot forward on right foot	⇧
31,32	Step left foot in place. Hitch right knee, scoot forward on left foot	
33	Touch right toe to right side	
34	Turn half turn right on left foot, stepping right foot beside left	◗
35,36	Touch left toe to left side. Step left foot beside right	
	Heel Switches, Heel Hook	
37&	Tap right heel forward. Step right foot beside left	○
38&	Tap left heel forward. Step left foot beside right	
39,40	Tap right heel forward. Hook right foot over left shin	

Beats	Movement	Direction
	Diagonal Steps, Toe Touches, Kick, Cross, Unwind, Clap	
41	Step right foot forward diagonally right	○
42	Touch left toe behind right foot	
43	Step left foot back diagonally left	
44	Touch right toe beside left foot	
45	Kick right foot forward diagonally right	
46	Cross right foot over left	
47,48	Unwind half turn left. Clap	◖

Begin again!

☆☆☆☆☆☆☆ Arumba ☆☆☆☆☆☆☆

Neil Hale, Pleasanton, USA — ***One Wall***

Beats	Movement	Direction
	Box Step	
1	Step left foot to left	⮤
2	Step right foot next to left	
3	Step left foot forward	
4	Hold	
5	Step right foot to right of left foot	⮧
6	Step left foot next to right	
7	Step right foot back	
8	Hold	

Beats	Movement	Direction
9	Step left foot to left of right foot	⇦
10	Step right foot next to left	
11	Step left foot to left into a quarter turn to left	◖
12	Hold	

Beats	Movement	Direction
	Rock and Return	
13	Rock step forward on right foot	❍
14	Step back on left foot	
15	Step right foot back into a quarter turn to right	◗
16	Step left foot next to right	

Beats	Movement	Direction
	Box Step	
17	Step right foot to right	
18	Step left foot next to right	
19	Step right foot forward	
20	Hold	
21	Step left foot to left of right foot	
22	Step right foot next to left	
23	Step left foot back	
24	Hold	
25	Step right foot to right of left foot	
26	Step left foot next to right	
27	Step right foot to right into a quarter turn to right	
28	Hold	
	Rock and Return	
29	Rock forward on left foot	
30	Step back on right foot	
31	Step left back into quarter turn to left	
32	Step right foot next to left	
33	Step left foot into a quarter turn left	
34	Hold	
35	Pivot half turn to left on ball of left foot while stepping around and back with right foot	

(Contd.)

Beats	Movement	Direction
36	Hold	
37	Step left foot back into a quarter turn to left	
38	Touch right foot next to left	
39	Step right foot to right side	
40	Step left next to right	
41	Step right foot into a quarter turn to right	
42	Hold	
43	Pivot half turn to right on ball of right foot while stepping around and back with left foot	
44	Hold	
45	Step right foot back into quarter turn to right	
46	Touch left foot next to right	
47	Step left foot to left	
48	Step right foot next to left	
	Move Left	
49	Step left foot to left	⇦
50	Hold and Clap	
51	Step right foot next to left	
52	Hold and clap	
53	Step left foot to left	

Beats	Movement	Direction
54	Hold and clap	
55	Touch right foot next to left	
56	Hold and clap	
	Move Right	
57	Step right foot to right side	⇨
58	Hold and clap	
59	Step left foot next to right	
60	Hold and clap	
61	Step right foot to right side	
62	Hold and clap	
63	Step left foot next to right	
64	Hold and clap	

Begin again!

☆☆☆☆☆ Big Ole Truck ☆☆☆☆☆

Sue Lipscombe, Bartlett, USA **_Four Wall_**

Beats	Movement	Direction
1	Turn both heels out	
2	Click heels together	
3	Touch right heel forward	
4	Step right foot in place	
5	Touch left heel forward	
6	Step left foot in place	
7	Click heels together	
8	Click heels together	
	Forward	
9	Step right foot forward at a 45-degree angle *(about 2 o'clock)*	
10	Touch left foot beside right and clap	
11	Step left foot forward at a 45-degree angle *(about 10 o'clock)*	
12	Touch right foot beside left and clap	
	Backward	
13	Step right foot back at a 45-degree angle *(about 5 o'clock)*	
14	Touch left foot beside right and clap	

Beats	Movement	Direction
15	Step left foot back at a 45-degree angle *(about 7 o'clock)*	
16	Step right foot beside left and clap	
	Hip Rolls	
17	Roll right hip to right *(begin moving hips in a counter-clockwise direction)*	
18	Roll left hip to left *(continuing the counter-clockwise roll)*	
19	Roll right hip to right *(a counter-clockwise circle again)*	
20	Roll left hip to left side *(end with weight on left foot)*	
	Right Sugar Foot	
21	Touch right toe beside left toe	
22	Touch right heel beside left toe	
23	Touch right toe beside left toe	
24	Touch right heel beside left toe	
	Right Vine	
25	Step right foot to right side	
26	Cross left foot behind right	
27	Step right foot to right side	
28	Kick left foot forward and clap	

(Contd.)

Beats	Movement	Direction
	Left Vine and Turn	
29	Step left foot to left side	
30	Cross right foot behind left	
31	Step left foot to left side	
32	Make a quarter turn to right, keeping right heel forward	
33	Touch right toe to right side	
34	Touch right toe behind left foot	
35	Touch right toe to right side	
36	Step right foot across left foot	
37	Touch left toe to left side	
38	Step left foot across right	
39	Touch right toe to right side	
40	Step right foot in place next to left	

Begin again!

☆☆☆☆☆☆ Black Coffee ☆☆☆☆☆☆

Helen O'Malley, Nash-Villains, Wicklow, Ireland **Four Wall**

Beats	Movement	Direction
	Flick Kicks and Shuffle-steps	
1–2	Kick right foot forward twice	○
3&4	Shuffle-step in place, right, left, right *(3 steps = 2 beats)*	
5–6	Kick left foot forward twice	
7&8	Shuffle-step in place, left, right, left *(3 steps = 2 beats)*	
	Paddle Turns	
9–10	Point right toe forward and pivot 1/8 turn to left	
11–12	Point right toe forward and pivot 1/8 turn to complete quarter turn left	◀
	Rock, Shuffle Half Turns and Heel Digs	
13–14	Rock forward on right foot, rock back on left	
15&16	Right shuffle-step, turning into a half turn right (ie, right, left, right)	◗
17–18	Rock forward on left foot, rock back on right foot	
19&20	Left shuffle-step turning into a half	◖

(Contd.)

Beats	Movement	Direction
	turn left (ie, left, right, left)	
21–22	Tap right heel forward, switch weight and tap left heel forward	❍
23–24	Switch weight and tap right heel forward and hold it there, clap hands	

Side Steps Right with Shoulder Shimmies or Hip Thrusts

Beats	Movement	Direction
25–26	Right steps to right side, shimmying shoulders at the same time	⇨
27–28	Close the left to the right and pause for one beat	
29–32	Repeat steps 25–28	

Left Vine with Scuff

Beats	Movement	Direction
33–34	Left foot steps to left side, cross right behind left	⇦
35–36	Left foot steps to left side, scuff the right foot in place	

Side Right, Pause and Finger Click

Beats	Movement	Direction
37–38	Right foot steps to right side, pause and click fingers shoulder high	⇨
39–40	Cross left foot behind right, pause and click fingers behind hips	
41–42	Right foot steps to right side, pause and click fingers shoulder high	

Beats	Movement	Direction
43–44	Cross left in front of right, pause and click fingers behind hips	⇨
	Pivot Turns – Left	
45–46	Step forward on right foot and pivot a half turn left	●
47–48	Step forward on right foot and pivot a half turn left	

Begin again!

☆☆☆☆ Breakin' the Bank ☆☆☆☆

Two-part Dance

Section 'A' is danced twice and Section 'B' once. Repeat pattern AAB until the music ends.

Beats	Movement	Direction
	SECTION A (Danced Twice)	
	Toe-Heel, Step, Stomp, Pigeon Toes	
1	Tap left toe beside right heel	❍
2	Tap left heel in front	
&	Step left foot beside right	
3	Tap right toe beside left heel	
4	Tap right heel front	
5,6	Stomp right foot beside left, twice	
7	Split heels apart	
8	Bring heels together	
	Travelling Pigeon Toes Right	
9	Heels still together, point toes out	⇨
&	Split heels apart	
10	Bring heels together, pointing toes out	
&	Split heels apart	
11	Bring heels together, pointing toes out	
&	Split heels apart	
12	Bring heels together, pointing toes out *(In order to travel on this step it is*	

Beats	Movement	Direction
	necessary to have weight on ball of one foot and heel of the other)	
	Vine Left	
13	Step left foot to left side	
14	Step right foot behind left	
15	Step left foot to left side	
16	Tap right toe behind	
	Charleston Step	
17	Step right foot forward	
18	Lift left knee	
19	Step left foot back	
20	Tap right toe behind	
	'Can-Can' Step	
21	Step right foot forward	
22–24	Lift left knee and shake boot for 3 counts	
	Step, Turn, Pivot, Knee Pops	
25	Step left foot back	
26	Step on right foot turning quarter turn right	
27	Step left foot forward	
28	Pivot half turn right	
29	Step left foot forward, pop right knee	

(Contd.)

Beats	Movement	Direction
30	Step right foot forward, pop left knee	⇧
31	Step left foot forward, pop right knee	
*32	Step right foot forward, pop left knee *(*When Section 'A' has been danced twice, say the word 'Break' on last count)*	
	SECTION B (Danced Once)	
1	Tap left toe to left side	❍
2	Step left foot beside right	
3	Tap right toe to right side	
4	Step right foot beside left	
5	Scuff left heel and kick left foot	
&	Step left foot down	
6	Step right foot beside left	
	Kick-Ball-Change, Quarter Turn Left	
7	Kick left foot forward	❍
&	Step left foot in place on ball of foot	
8	Step right foot beside left	
9	Touch left toe beside right heel	
10	Pivot quarter turn left	◖
11–22	Repeat Kick-Ball-Change pattern steps 7–10, 3 more times	

Begin again!

☆☆☆☆☆☆☆☆☆ Bubba ☆☆☆☆☆☆☆☆☆

Bill and Donna Hodel, Port Orange, USA ***Two Wall***

Beats	Movement	Direction
	Heel Splits	
1	Keeping weight on balls of feet, swing heels out in opposite directions	❍
2	Bring heels back	
3	Swing heels out again	
4	Bring heels back	
	Charlestons	
5	Touch right heel front	❍
6	Touch right toe back	
7	Step forward on right	
8	Kick left foot forward	
9	Step back on left	
10	Touch right toe back	
11	Step forward on right	
12	Kick left foot forward	
13	Step back on left	
14	Place right foot beside left	
	Swivels	
15	With weight on balls of feet, turn heels to right	⇨
16	With weight on heels, turn toes to right	

(Contd.)

Beats	Movement	Direction
17	With weight on balls of feet, turn heels to right	⇨
18	With weight on heels, turn toes to centre	
	Three Hitches and Turns	
19	Step with right foot, turning a quarter turn to right	
20	Hitch left leg (raise left knee)	
21	Step with left foot, turning a quarter turn to right	
22	Hitch right leg (raise right knee)	
23	Step with right foot, turning a quarter turn to right	
24	Hitch left leg (raise left knee)	
25	Step forward on left	⇧
26	Step forward on right	
27	Hitch left leg, scoot forward on right	
28	Scoot forward on right again (while scooting forward, hold hands as if you were firing guns)	
29	Step forward on left	
30	Step forward on right	
31	Step left, doing a quarter turn to left	
32	Stomp right foot next to left	
	Begin again!	

☆☆☆☆ Bump in the Dark ☆☆☆☆

Jo Thompson, Nashville, USA — ***Four Wall***

Beats	Movement	Direction
	Step to Side, Touch	
1,2	Step right foot to right side, touch left toe beside right	❍
3,4	Step left foot to left side, touch right toe beside left	
5–8	Repeat steps 1–4	
	Rock Steps Forward and Back	
9&	Rock right foot in front of left, step left foot in place	❍
10&	Rock right foot behind left, step left foot in place	
11&	Rock right foot in front of left, step left foot in place	
12	Step right foot in place	
	Repeat steps 9–12 with left foot leading . . .	❍
13&	Rock left foot in front of right, step right foot in place	
14&	Rock left foot behind right, step right foot in place	

(Contd.)

Beats	Movement	Direction
15&	Rock left foot in front of right, step right foot in place	
16	Step left foot in place	
	Rock Right, Rock Left	
17&	Rock right foot in front of left, step left foot in place	○
18	Step right foot beside left	
19&	Rock left foot in front of right, step right foot in place	
20	Step left foot in place	
	Half Turns	
21,22	Step right foot forward, pivot half turn left	●
23,24	Repeat steps 21,22	
	Basketball Turns (quarter L, half R, half L) and Jumping Jack	
25	Pivot quarter turn left, touching right foot to right side	◔
26	Pivot half turn right, touching right foot to right side	◗
27	Pivot half turn left, touching right foot to right side	◖
&28	Jump, crossing right foot over left. Jump feet apart	

Beats	Movement	Direction
	Basketball Turns (half R, half L, half R) and Jumping Jack	
29	Pivot half turn right, touching right foot to right side	◗
30	Pivot half turn left, touching right foot to right side	◖
31	Pivot half turn right, touching right foot to right side	◗
&32	Jump, crossing left foot over right. Jump feet apart *(now facing 3 o'clock)*	
	Hip Bumps	
33,34	Bump hips left, right	○
35&36	Bump hips left, right, left	
	Half Turn, Stomp	
37,38	Step right foot forward. Pivot half turn left	◖
39,40	Stomp right foot in place. Stomp left foot in place	

Begin again!

☆☆☆☆☆ The Cajun Queen ☆☆☆☆☆

Anne Fore, Salem, USA — ***One Wall***

Beats	Movement	Direction
1	Touch right heel forward diagonally	⇨
2	With weight on ball of left foot, swivel left heel to right and touch right toe next to left foot	
3	Switch weight to left heel, swivel left toe to right and touch right heel forward diagonally	
4	Touch right heel beside left	
	Heel Taps	
5	Touch right heel forward	❍
6	Step right foot next to left	
7	Touch left heel forward	
8	Step left foot beside right	
	Heel-Ball-Change	
9	Touch right heel forward	❍
&	Step right foot in place, lift left foot slightly	
10	Step left foot in place	
11	Touch right heel forward	
12	Touch right toe next to left	

Beats	Movement	Direction
	Right Vine	
13	Step right foot to right	⇨
14	Step left foot behind right	
15	Step right foot to right	
16	Scuff left foot	
	Left Vine	
17	Step left foot to left	⇦
18	Step right foot behind left	
19	Step left foot to left	
20	Make half turn to left, swing right leg around	◖
	Right Vine	
21	Step right foot to right	⇨
22	Step left foot behind right	
23	Step right foot to right	
24	Stomp left foot next to right	
	Swivet	
25	With weight on left heel and right toe, fan left toe to left and right heel to right *(both toes end up pointing to left)*	❍
26	Centre feet *(left toe to right, right heel to left)*	
27	With weight on left heel and right toe, fan left toe to left and right heel to right	

(Contd.)

Beats	Movement	Direction
28	Centre feet	○
29	With weight on right heel and left toe, fan right toe to right and left heel to left *(both toes end up pointing to right)*	
30	Centre feet	
31	Step right foot over left	
32	Make half turn to left, unwinding legs	◖

Begin again!

☆☆☆☆☆ The Cajun Slap ☆☆☆☆☆

Four Wall

Beats	Movement	Direction
	Right Vine	
1	Step out to the right with right foot	⇨
2	Step behind right with left foot	
3	Step out again with right foot	
4	Touch left foot next to right	
5	Touch left toe out to left side	❍
6	Touch toe next to right foot	
7	Touch left toe out again	
8	Touch toe next to right foot	
	Left Vine	
9	Step out to the left with left foot	⇦
10	Step behind left with right foot	
11	Step out again with left foot	
12	Touch right foot next to left	
13	Touch right toe out to right side	❍
14	Touch toe next to left foot	
15	Touch right toe out again	
16	Step right next to left	

(Contd.)

Beats	Movement	Direction
	Prances	
17	Turn left toe in and touch slightly in front	❍
18	Step back home	
19	Turn right toe in and touch slightly in front	
20	Step back home	
21	Turn left toe in and touch slightly in front	
22	Step back home	
23	Turn right toe in and touch slightly in front	
24	Step back home	
25,26	Touch left heel in front twice	❍
27,28	Touch left toe back twice	
	Slaps	
29	Hitch (raise) left knee and slap with left hand	❍
30	Stomp left foot down *(don't switch weight)*	
31	Cross left foot in front of right knee, slap boot with right hand	
32	Stomp left foot down *(don't switch weight)*	

33 Step forward with left foot ⇧
34 Drag right foot to meet left
35 Step forward with left foot
36 Hitch (raise) right knee, making quarter turn to left ◖

---

37 Touch right toe to right side ○
38 Bring right foot up behind left knee, slap right boot with left hand
39 Touch right toe out again
40 Touch right foot next to left

Begin again!

☆☆☆☆☆ California Coast ☆☆☆☆☆

Four Wall

Beats	Movement	Direction
	Hip Bumps	
1	Step right foot forward diagonally, bumping hips to right	❍
&2	Bump hips, left, right	
3&4	Bump hips diagonally back to left twice *(weight on left foot)*	
5	Step right foot back diagonally, bumping hips to right	❍
&6	Bump hips to back, left, right	
7&8	Bump hips forward diagonally to left twice *(weight on left foot)*	
	Modified Right Vine with Star	
9	Step right foot to right side	⇨
10	Step left foot behind right	
11	Step right foot to right side	
12	Point left toe forward	❍
13	Point left toe out to left side	
14	Point left toe way back	

Beats	Movement	Direction
	Modified Left Vine	
15	Step left foot to left side	
16	Step right foot behind left	
17	Step left foot to left side	
	Pivot Turns	
18	Step right foot forward	
19	Pivot half turn left	
20,21	Repeat steps 18,19	
	Quarter Turn	
22	Step right foot forward	
23	Kick left foot out to left side	
24	Swing left leg around, making quarter turn right, and end with feet crossed left over right *(weight on left foot)*	

Begin again!

☆☆☆☆ Caribbean Cowboy ☆☆☆☆

Ed Henry — ***Two Wall***

Beats	Movement	Direction
	Side, Together, Side, Together, Side, Together, Side, Touch	
1,2	Step right foot to right side. Step left foot beside right	⇨
3–6	Repeat steps 1,2 twice	
7,8	Step right foot to right side. Touch left foot beside right	
9,10	Step left foot to left side. Step right foot beside left	⇦
11–14	Repeat 9,10 twice	
15,16	Step left foot to left side. Touch right foot beside left	
	Shimmy Right, Shimmy Left	
17	Step right foot to right side *(big step)*	⇨
18,19	Slide left to meet right, shimmy shoulders	
20	Step left foot beside right, taking weight on left	
21–24	Repeat steps 17–20	
25	Step left foot to left side *(big step)*	⇦
26,27	Slide right to meet left, shimmy shoulders	
28	Step right foot beside left, taking	

Beats	Movement	Direction
	weight on right	
29–32	Repeat steps 25–28	
	Swivet	
	With weight on left heel and right toe . . .	
33,34	Pivot feet left, centre	○
35–40	Repeat steps 33,34, three more times	
	With weight on right heel and left toe . . .	
41,42	Pivot feet right, centre	
43–48	Repeat steps 41,42, three more times	
	Rock Back, Shuffle	
49,50	Rock back onto right foot. Step left foot in place	○
51&52	Shuffle in place, right, left, right	
53,54	Rock back onto left foot. Step right foot in place	
55&56	Shuffle in place, left, right, left	
	Kick-Ball-Change, Unwind, Bump Hips	
57	Kick right foot forward	○
&	Step on ball of right foot	
58	Step left foot in place	
59	Cross right foot over left	
60	Unwind half turn left	◖
61–64	Bump hips right, left, right, left	
	Begin again!	

☆☆☆☆☆ Cha-Cha Maria ☆☆☆☆☆

Joan O'Gorman, Dublin, Ireland — ***Two Wall***

If you already know Elvira, *you know most of this dance because steps 9 through 24 are the same.*

Beats	Movement	Direction
1	Step right foot forward on ball of foot	⇧
2	Step right foot down	
3	Step left foot forward on ball of foot	
4	Step left foot down	
5,6	Kick right foot forward twice	
7	Step right foot directly back	
8	Step left foot forward	
	Shuffle Half Turn, Shuffle Quarter Turn	
9&10	Shuffle forward, right, left, right	⇧
11	Step left foot forward	
12	Pivot half turn right	◗
13&14	Shuffle forward, left, right, left	⇧
15	Step right foot forward	
16	Pivot quarter turn left	◖
	Half Turn, Shuffle, Half Turn, Shuffle	
17	Step right foot forward	
18	Pivot half turn left	◖

Beats	Movement	Direction
19&20	Shuffle forward, right, left, right	⇧
21	Step left foot forward	
22	Pivot half turn right	◗
23&24	Shuffle forward, left, right, left	⇧
25	Cross right foot over left, stepping on ball of foot	
26	Step right foot down	
27	Step left foot back, stepping on ball of foot	⇩
28	Step left foot down	
29	Touch right toe back	
30	Swivel quarter turn right, switching weight to right foot	◣
31	Stomp left foot	
32	Stomp right foot *(no weight on stomp)*	❍

Begin again!

☆☆ Church Street Station Stomp ☆☆

Kip Sweeney, Orlando, USA — ***Four Wall***

Beats	Movement	Direction
	Right Vine	
1	Step right foot to right side	⇨
2	Step left foot behind right	
3	Step right foot to right side	
4	Stomp left foot and clap	
	Left Vine	
5	Step left foot to left side	⇦
6	Step right foot behind left	
7	Step left foot to left side	
8	Stomp right foot and clap	
	Back Walk	
9	Step right foot back	⇩
10	Step left foot back	
11	Step right foot back	
12	Stomp left foot and clap	
	Stomps	
13	Step left foot forward	○
14	Stomp right foot next to left and clap	
15	Step right foot back	
16	Tap left toe next to right foot	

Beats	Movement	Direction
17	Step left foot forward	❍
18,19	Stomp right next to left twice and clap	
20	Hold	
21	Step right foot back	
22	Tap left toe next to right foot	
	Shuffle-steps	
23&24	Left shuffle-step forward (left, right, left)	⇧
25&26	Right shuffle-step forward (right, left, right)	
27&28	Left shuffle-step forward (left, right, left)	
	Right Vine	
29–32	Repeat steps 1–4	⇨
	Left Vine	
33–36	Repeat steps 5–8	⇦
	Step and Stomps	
37	Step right foot forward	❍
38	Stomp left foot next to right and clap	
39	Step left foot forward	
40	Stomp right foot next to left and clap	

(Contd.)

Beats	Movement	Direction
	Back Walks	
41	Step right foot back	⇩
42	Step left foot back	
43	Step right foot back, making quarter turn to right	◔
44	Stomp left foot and clap	
45	Step left foot to left	❍
46	Stomp right foot next to left and clap	
47	Step right foot to right	
48	Stomp left foot next to right and clap	
	Tush Push	
49	Step forward on left foot, pushing left hip forward	❍
50	Push right hip back	
51	Push left hip forward	
52	Push right hip back	
53	Make half turn clockwise to right, switching weight to left foot and swinging right leg around	◗
54	Hitch right leg, raising knee	

Begin again!

☆☆☆☆☆ Cimmeron Boogie ☆☆☆☆☆

Two Wall

May also be dance in opposing lines.

Beats	Movement	Direction
	Heel Touch, Heel Close	
1	Tap left heel forward	❍
2	Touch left foot beside right	
3	Tap left heel forward	
4	Step left foot beside right	
	Repeat steps 1–4 on right foot . . .	
5	Tap right heel forward	❍
6	Touch right foot beside left	
7	Tap right heel forward	
8	Step right foot beside left	
	Heel Swivels and Hook	
9	Swivel heels right	❍
10	Swivel heels centre	
11	Swivel heels left	
12	Swivel heels centre	
13	Tap right heel forward	
14	Hook right foot over left shin	
15,16	Repeat steps 13,14	

(Contd.)

Beats	Movement	Direction
	Right Vine	
17	Step right foot to right side	⇨
18	Step left foot behind right	
19	Step right foot to right side	
20	Kick left foot behind right	❍
21	Tap left heel forward	
22	Hook left foot over right shin	
	Left Vine	
23	Step left foot to left side	⇦
24	Step right foot behind left	
25	Step left foot to left side	
26	Kick right foot forward	
	Walk Backward	
27	Step right foot back	⇩
28	Step left foot back	
29	Step right foot back	
30	Kick left foot forward	
	Shuffles Forward and Backward	
31&32	Shuffle forward left, right, left	⇧
33&34	Shuffle forward right, left, right, turning half turn left	◖
35&36	Shuffle back left, right, left	
37&38	Shuffle back right, left, right	⇩

Begin again!

☆☆☆☆☆ The Cinderella ☆☆☆☆☆

Judy and Cathy Lee, Boca Raton, USA **_Two Wall_**

Beats	Movement	Direction
	Heel Swivels	
1	With feet together, swivel heels right	❍
2	Swivel heels centre	
3–4	Repeat steps 1–2	
5	Swivel heels left	❍
6	Swivel heels centre	
7–8	Repeat steps 5–6	
9	Swivel heels right	❍
10	Swivel heels left	
11–12	Repeat steps 9–10	
	Shuffle-steps and Turns	
13&14	Shuffle-step forward, stepping right, left, right	⇧
15&16	Shuffle-step forward, stepping left, right, left	
17	Step right foot forward	
18	Make half turn to left	◖
19–24	Repeat steps 13–18	

(Contd.)

Beats	Movement	Direction
	Knee Pops	
25	Lift right heel so that right knee pops forward	❍
26	Lower right heel, lift left heel so that left knee pops forward	
27–32	Repeat steps 25–26 three more times	
33	Jump back, landing on left foot with right heel diagonal forward	❍
34	Jump, bringing feet together	
35	Jump back, landing on right foot with left heel diagonal forward	
36	Jump, bringing feet together	
37–40	Repeat steps 33–36	
	Jump Turn	
41	Jump, landing with feet apart	
42	Jump, landing with right foot crossing left leg	
43	Unwind legs, making half turn to left	◖
44	Hold and clap	
	Shoulder Rolls	
45–46	Roll right shoulder back	❍
47–48	Roll left shoulder back	

Beats	Movement	Direction
	Slow Forward Walk	
49	Step forward on ball of right foot	⇧
50	Lower right heel	
51	Step forward on ball of left foot	
52	Lower left heel	
53–56	Repeat steps 49–52	
57	Touch right toe next to left foot	○
58	Tap right heel forward	
59	Step right foot across left foot	
60	Hold and clap	
61	Touch left toe next to right foot	○
62	Tap left heel forward	
63	Step left foot across right foot	
64	Hold and clap	
65	Kick right foot forward	⇩
66	Step right foot back	
67	Kick left foot forward	
68	Step left foot back	
69–72	Repeat steps 65–68	
	Step Drags	
73	Step right foot forward	⇧
74	Drag left foot next to right	
75	Step right foot forward	

(Contd.)

Beats	Movement	Direction
76	Drag left foot forward and scuff past right	⇧
77	Step left foot forward	
78	Drag right foot next to left	
79	Step left foot forward	
80	Stomp right foot next to left	

Begin again!

☆☆ CMT's Dance Ranch Romp ☆☆

Jo Thompson, Nashville, USA — ***Four Wall***

Beats	Movement	Direction
	Heel Grinds and Rock Steps	
1	Step right forward with weight on right heel only and right toe turned in; grind heel into floor, turning toes to right	○
2	Step left in place	
3	Rock back slightly on ball of right foot	
4	Step left in place	
5–8	Repeat steps 1–4	
	Turns	
9	Step right foot forward	
10	Pivot half turn to left, shifting weight to left foot	◖
11	Step right foot forward	
12	Pivot half turn to left, shifting weight to left foot	◖
	Stomps and Heel Stand	
13	Stomp right foot next to left and switch weight to right	○
14	Stomp left foot next to right, bending knees slightly	

(Contd.)

Beats	Movement	Direction
15	Straightening legs, lift toes of both feel slightly off floor *(optional: Whoo!)*	❍
16	Lower toes to floor	

	Right Vine with Romp	
17	Step right foot to right	⇨
18	Step left foot behind right foot	
19	Step right foot to right	
20	Touch ball of left foot next to right, turning body slightly to right	
&21	Step left diagonally back and then touch right heel to floor diagonally forward	❍
&22	Step right in original position and touch ball of left foot next to right	
&23	Step left diagonally back and then touch right heel to floor diagonally forward	
&24	Step right in original position and touch ball of left foot next to right	

	Left Vine with Romp	
25	Step left foot to left	⇦
26	Step right foot behind left foot	
27	Step left foot to left	
28	Touch ball of right foot next to left, turning body slightly to left	

Beats	Movement	Direction
&29	Step right diagonally back and touch left heel to floor diagonally forward	○
&30	Step left in original position and touch ball of right foot next to left	
&31	Step right diagonally back and touch left heel to floor diagonally forward	
&32	Step left in original position and touch ball of right foot next to left	
	Step Scoots	
33	Step right foot forward	⇧
34	Raise left knee and scoot forward on right foot	
35	Step left foot back	⇩
36	Step right foot next to left	
37	Step left foot forward	
38	Raise right knee and scoot forward on left foot	⇧
39	Step right foot back	⇩
40	Step left foot next to right	
41	Step right foot forward	
42	Raise left knee and scoot forward on right foot	⇧
	Box Step with Quarter Turn	
43	Step left across in front of right	
44	Step right foot back	

(Contd.)

Beats	Movement	Direction
45	Step left foot to left side and make quarter turn to left	◖
46	Stomp right foot slightly ahead of left *(do not switch weight)*	
47	Brush hands – right goes down as left comes up	❍
48	Brush hands again – left goes down as right comes up	

Begin again!

☆☆☆☆ Cotton County Queen ☆☆☆☆

Parry Spence, Nashville, USA **_One Wall_**

Beats	Movement	Direction
	Jump, Cross, Jump, Together	
1	With feet shoulder-width apart, jump back slightly on left foot and tap right heel forward to right	○
2	Jump back to centre, crossing left foot over right foot	
3	Jump back slightly on right foot and tap left heel forward to left	
4	Jump back to centre with feet together	
	Quarter Turns	
5	Touch right toe forward	
6	Roll hips to make quarter turn left	
7	Touch right toe forward	
8	Roll hips to make quarter turn left, bring feet together and clap	
	Heel Scuffs	
9	Scuff right heel forward	⇧
&	Hitch right foot up across front of left shin	
10	Step down on right foot, crossing over left foot	

(Contd.)

Beats	Movement	Direction
11	Scuff left heel forward	⇧
&	Hitch left foot up across front of right shin	
12	Step down on left foot, crossing over right foot	
	Butterfly	
13,14	Turn heels out to sides and return to centre	❍
	Chug and Clap	
15	Chug forward (small jump with both feet)	⇧
16	Clap	
	Shuffle-steps	
	(Hands on buckle, shoulders rocking with steps)	
17&18	With a quarter turn to right, right shuffle-step forward (right, left, right)	◔
19&20	Left shuffle-step forward (left, right, left)	
	Kick, Flip, Stomp, Clap	
21	Kick right foot forward	
22	Make half turn to left on left foot, keeping right knee bent with foot kicked up behind	◖

Beats	Movement	Direction
23	Stomp right foot next to left	❍
24	Clap	
25–32	Repeat steps 17–24	
	Cross, Turn, Roll, Clap	
33	Cross right foot behind left foot (plant right toe)	
34	Make half turn to right with weight on left foot	◗
35&36	Roll hip up to right, clap	❍
37	Cross right foot behind left foot (plant right toe)	
38	Make half turn to right with weight on left foot	◗
39&40	Roll hip up to right, clap	❍

Begin again!

☆☆☆☆ Countdown Shuffle ☆☆☆☆

Max Perry, Danbury, USA — *Four Wall*

Beats	Movement	Direction
	Jazz Jump Back, Walk Forward	
&1,2	Jump back on right foot then left, clap	⇩
&3,4	Repeat &1,2	
5,6,7	Walk forward, right, left right	⇧
&8	Kick left foot forward, step left foot beside right	
	Side Touches	
9,10	Touch right toe to right side. Step right foot in place	○
11,12	Touch left toe to left side. Step left foot in place	
	Chassé Right	
13&	Step right foot to right side. Step left foot beside right	⇨
14&	Step right foot to right side. Step left foot beside right	
15,16	Step right foot to right side. Touch left foot beside right	
	Right Left *(Max says 'With Attitude!')*	
17	Step left foot to left side	⇦

Beats	Movement	Direction
18	Step right foot behind left	⇦
19	Step left to left side, pushing hips left	
&20	Push hips right then left	
	Doubles	
21,22	Tap right heel forward twice	○
23,24	Tap right toe back twice	
	Quarter Turn x 4	
25	Step right foot forward	
26	Turn quarter turn left	◖
27–32	Repeat steps 25,26 three more times	
	Diamond Shuffle	
	(Face 1 o'clock)	
33–36	Shuffle forward right, left, right (1&2) Shuffle forward left, right, left (3&4)	⬀
	(Face 4 o'clock)	
37–40	Shuffle back right, left, right (1&2) Shuffle back left, right, left (3&4)	⬂
	(Face 7 o'clock)	
41–44	Shuffle forward right, left, right (1&2) Shuffle forward left, right, left (3&4)	⬀
	(Face 9 o'clock)	
45–48	Shuffle back right, left, right (1&2) Shuffle back left, right, left (3&4)	⇩

Begin again!

☆☆☆☆☆ The Cow Boogie ☆☆☆☆☆

Donna Wasnick, Tulare, USA **Four Wall**

Beats	Movement	Direction
	After 32-count song intro.	
	Touch Steps	
1	Tap right toe next to left foot	❍
2	Step right heel down	
3	Tap left toe next to right foot	
4	Step left heel down	
5	Tap right toe to right side	
6	Step right foot next to left	
7	Tap left toe to left side	
8	Step left foot next to right	
	Step and Snap to Right	
9	Step right to right side and swing hands out to right side	⇨
10	Hold foot position and snap fingers down to right side	
11	Hook left toe behind right foot and swing hands out to left side	
12	Step down on left heel and snap fingers down to left side	
13–16	Repeat steps 9–12	

Beats	Movement	Direction
	Toe-Heel-Fan-Clap	
17	Turning right knee inward, touch right toe next to left	
18	Step right heel down	
19	Fan right toe to right at an angle, body follows	
20	Hold and clap	
21	Turning left knee inward, touch left toe next to right	
22	Step left heel down	
23	Fan left toe to left at an angle, body follows	
24	Hold and clap	
	Three-quarter Turn	
25	Cross right in front of left	
26	Begin three-quarter turn to left on ball of left foot	
27,28	Complete turn to left, sink heels down with feet next to each other, hold	
	Boogie Down and Boogie Up	
29–30	Boogie down: Twist heels and hips left, right	
31–32	Boogie up: Twist heels and hips left, centre	

Begin again!

☆☆☆☆ Cowboy Hand Jive ☆☆☆☆

Neil Hale, Pleasanton, USA **_Four Wall_**

Begin after 16-count intro if using I'm A Cowboy *by The Smokin' Armadillos.*

Beats	Movement	Direction
	Point, Touch, Point and Step, Touch	
1,2	Touch right toe to right side. Touch right toe beside left	❍
3	Touch right toe to right side	
&4	Step right foot beside left. Touch left toe beside right	
5,6	Touch left toe to left side. Touch left toe beside right	
7	Touch left toe to left side	
&8	Step left foot beside right. Touch right toe beside left	
	Heel, Touch, Heel and Step, Touch	
9,10	Touch right heel forward. Touch right toe beside left	❍
11	Touch right heel forward	
&12	Step right foot beside left. Touch left toe beside right	
13,14	Touch left heel forward. Touch left toe beside right	
15	Touch left heel forward	

Beats	Movement	Direction
&16	Step left foot beside right. Touch right toe beside left	○
	Stomp, Back, Back and Together, Forward	
17	Stomp right foot forward with foot angled to left	○
18,19	Step left foot back. Step right foot back	
&20	Step left foot beside right. Step right foot forward	
21	Stomp left foot forward with foot angled to right	
22,23	Step right foot back. Step left foot back	
&24	Step right foot beside left. Step left foot forward	
25–32	Repeat steps 17–24	
	Shuffles and Pivots	
33&34	Shuffle in place, right, left, right	◖
&	Pivot half turn left (turns are tight)	
35&36	Shuffle in place, left, right, left	
&	Pivot quarter turn right	◣
37&38	Shuffle in place, right, left, right	
&	Pivot half turn left	◖
39&40	Shuffle in place, left, right, left	

(Contd.)

Beats	Movement	Direction
	'Cowboy Hand Jive'	
41	Cross right foot over left	O
&	Swing left leg up behind right, slap left heel with right hand	
42,43	Step left foot back slightly, step right foot to right side	
&44	Brush-slap hips bring hands forward, clap in front	
45	Cross left foot over right	
&	Swing right leg up behind left, slap right heel with left hand	
46,47	Step right foot back slightly, step left foot to left side	
&48	Brush-slap hips bringing hands forward, clap in front	

Begin again!

☆☆☆☆☆ Cowboy Rhythm ☆☆☆☆☆

Jo Thompson, Nashville, USA

Four Wall

Beats	Movement	Direction
	Stomp and Toe Fans	
1	Stomp right foot slightly in front of left, toes pointed in, heel out	❍
2	Fan right toes out	
3	Fan right toes in	
4	Fan right toes out	
	Repeat steps 1–4 on left foot . . .	
5	Stomp left foot slightly in front of right, toes pointed in, heel out	❍
6	Fan left toes out	
7	Fan left toes in	
8	Fan left toes out	
	Stomps and Slap Leather	
9	Stomp right foot out to right side	❍
10	Stomp left foot out to left side . . . feet shoulder width apart	
11	Swing right leg behind left, slap right boot with left hand	
12	Step right foot down	
13	Swing left leg behind right, slap left	

(Contd.)

Beats	Movement	Direction
	boot with right hand	○
14	Step left foot down . . . feet still apart	
15,16	Clap hands, twice	
	Side Steps and Pigeon Toes	
17	Step right foot to right side	⇨
18	Step left foot beside right	
19	Swing heels out	○
20	Swing heels in	
	Repeat steps 17–20 on left foot . . .	
21	Step left foot to left side	⇦
22	Step right foot beside left	
23	Swing heels out	○
24	Swing heels in	
	Diagonal Steps Backward and Clap	
25	Step right foot back diagonally *(angle body)*	⇘
26	Clap	
27	Step left foot back diagonally *(angle body)*	⇙
28	Clap	
29-32	Repeat steps 25–28	
	Right Vine	
33	Step right foot to right side	⇨

Beats	Movement	Direction
34	Step left foot behind right	⇨
35	Step right foot to right side	
36	Scuff left foot forward	
	Left Vine	
37	Step left foot to left side	⇦
38	Step right foot behind left	
39	Step left foot to left side	
40	Scuff right foot forward	
	Scuff Steps Forward	
41	Step right foot forward	⇧
42	Scuff left foot forward	
43	Step left foot forward	
44	Scuff right foot forward	
45	Step right foot forward	
46	Scuff left foot forward	
47	Step left foot forward making quarter turn left	◾
48	Scuff right foot forward	

Begin again!

☆☆☆☆☆☆ Crazy Legs ☆☆☆☆☆☆

Greg Underwood, USA — ***Four Wall***

Beats	Movement	Direction
	Stomp, Kick, Cross, Kick, Out, Kick, Cross, Side Steps, Slide, Stomp	
1	Stomp right foot beside left	❍
&	Low kick right foot forward	
2	Bending knees, hook right foot over left shin	
&	Straighten legs, low kick right foot forward	
3	Bending knees, swing right foot out to right side	
&	Straighten legs, low kick right foot forward	
4	Bending knees, hook right foot over left shin	
5	Step right foot to right side	⇨
&	Step left foot beside right	
6	Step right foot to right side	
7	Slide left foot up to meet right	
&	Stomp left foot beside right	❍
8	Stomp right foot in place	

Repeat steps 1–8 with left foot leading . . .

Beats	Movement	Direction
9	Stomp left foot beside right	❍
&	Low kick left foot forward	
10	Bending knees, hook left foot over right shin	
&	Straighten legs, low kick left foot forward	
11	Bending knees swing left foot out to left side	
&	Straighten legs, low kick left foot forward	
12	Bending knees, hook left foot over right shin	
13	Step left foot to left side	⇦
&	Step right foot beside left	
14	Step left foot to left side	
15	Slide right foot up to meet left	
&	Stomp right foot beside left	❍
16	Stomp left foot in place	
	Right Shuffle, Half Turn, Left Shuffle, Half Turn	
17	Step right foot forward	⇧
&	Step let foot beside right	
18	Step left foot forward	
19	Step left foot forward	
20	Pivot half turn right	◗
21	Step left foot forward	

(Contd.)

Beats	Movement	Direction
&	Step right foot beside left	⇧
22	Step left foot forward	
23	Step right foot forward	
24	Pivot half turn left	◖

Together, Out, Out, Twist, Point Right, Left, Heel, Toe

Beats	Movement	Direction
25	Step right foot beside left	❍
&	Step left foot to left side	
26	Step right foot to right side, point toes out slightly (weight now on both feet)	
27	Bending knees, twist both toes in	
&	Twist both heels in	
28	Twist both toes in	
29	Point right toe to right side	
&	Step right foot beside left	❍
30	Point left toe to left side	
&	Step left foot beside right	
31	Tap right heel forward	
&	Step right foot beside left	
32	Touch left toe back	

Knee Lifts, Steps, Turns, Twists

Beats	Movement	Direction
33	Bending left leg, lift left knee up and forward	❍
34	Low kick left foot back	
35	Lift left knee up again	

Beats	Movement	Direction
&	Step left foot back	◯
36	Step right foot forward	
37	Step left foot forward	
38	Pivot half turn left	◖
39	Step left foot forward	
&	Pivot quarter turn right on balls of both feet twisting heels left	◗
40	Twist heels right *(end with weight on left foot to begin again)*	

Begin again!

☆☆☆☆☆☆☆☆ Cruisin' ☆☆☆☆☆☆☆☆

Neil Hale, Pleasanton, USA **_One Wall_**

For the 'Cha-Cha in place' steps, dance 3 steps in 2 beats on the spot.

Beats	Movement	Direction
	Rock Steps	
1	Rock left foot across right	○
2	Rock onto right foot in place	
3&4	Cha-Cha in place . . . left, right, left	
5	Rock right foot across left	○
6	Rock onto left foot in place	
7&8	Cha-Cha in place . . . right, left, right	
9	Rock left foot forward	○
10	Rock back onto right foot	
11&12	Cha-Cha in place . . . left, right, left	
13	Rock right foot back	○
14	Rock onto left foot in place	
15&16	Cha-Cha in place . . . right, left, right	
	Pivot Turns	
17	Step left foot forward	●
18	Pivot half turn to right	
19,20	Repeat steps 17, 18	

Beats	Movement	Direction
	Figure-eight Vine	
21	Step left foot to left side	
22	Step right foot behind left	
23	Step left foot making quarter turn to left	
24	Step right foot forward	
25	Pivot three-quarter turn left to face original wall	
26	Step right foot to right side	
27	Step left foot behind right	
28	Step right foot making quarter turn to right	
29	Step left foot forward	
30	Pivot half turn right	
31	Step left foot forward	
32	Pivot quarter turn right to face original wall	

Begin again!

☆☆☆☆☆ Daddy's Money ☆☆☆☆☆

Carol Weiner-Hamm, Pittsburgh, USA | **_Two Wall_**

Beats	Movement	Direction
	Shuffle-steps	
1&2	Shuffle-step forward beginning with right foot (right, left, right)	⇧
3&4	Shuffle-step forward (left, right left)	
5	Step right foot forward	⇧
6	Scoot on right foot and hitch (lift) left knee	
7	Step left foot forward	
8	Scoot on left foot and hitch right knee	
	Syncopated Out and In	
&9	Step right foot out to right and step left foot out to left	○
&10	Step right foot to centre and step left foot to centre	
11	Rock forward on right foot	
12	Rock back on left foot	
13	Step right foot diagonally back to right	○
14	Raise left knee, keeping toes on floor	
15–16	Push hips forward twice while swinging right hand at hip level	

Beats	Movement	Direction
	Pivot Turns	
17	Step left foot forward	
18	Make half turn to right, switching weight to right foot	◗
19,20	Repeat steps 17,18	
	Jazz Box	
21	Cross step left foot over right	○
22	Step right foot back	
23	Step left foot to left	
24	Touch right foot next to left	
	Monterey Turns	
25	Touch right toe out to right	
26	Make half turn to right on left foot, swinging right foot around and stepping next to left	◗
27	Touch left foot out to left	
28	Step left foot next to right	
29–32	Repeat steps 25–28	
	Slow Merengue Half Turn	
33	Step right foot to right, making 1/8 turn	◗
34	Step left foot next to right and clap	
35–40	Repeat steps 33,34 3 times	

Begin again!

☆☆☆☆☆ Dancin' Hearts ☆☆☆☆☆

Bubs Jewell, Caboolture, Australia **Four Wall**

Beats	Movement	Direction
	Cross Rock Steps	
1	Step left foot forward 45 degrees to right *(diagonal in front of left foot)*	❍
2	Rock back on right foot	
3	Step left foot next to right	
4	Step right foot forward 45 degrees to left *(diagonal in front of right foot)*	❍
5	Rock back on left foot	
6	Step right foot next to left	
7	Step left foot forward 45 degrees to right	❍
8	Rock back on right foot	
9	Step left foot next to right	
10	Pivot on ball of left foot, make half turn to left, and step with right foot	◖
11	Step left foot next to right	
12	Step right foot in place	
13–24	Repeat steps 1–12	
	Waltz Steps with Turn	
25	Step left forward and half turn to left	⇧

Beats	Movement	Direction
26	Step right foot next to left, completing turn	◖
27	Step left foot in place	
28	Step right foot back	⇩
29	Step left foot next to right	
30	Step right foot in place	
31–36	Repeat steps 25–30	
	Right Vine	
37	Step left foot in front of right	⇨
38	Step right foot to right side	
39	Step left foot behind right	
40	Step right foot to right side	
41	Step left foot in front of right	
42	Step right foot to right side	
	Left Monterey Turn	
43	Touch left foot to left side, keeping weight on right foot	
44	Make half turn to left on right foot, swinging left foot around and stepping next to right	◖
45	Touch right foot to right side	
46	Step right foot next to left	○
47	Step left foot in place	

(Contd.)

Beats	Movement	Direction
48	Step right foot in place	
49–54	Repeat steps 37–42 *(Right Vine)*	
55–60	Repeat steps 43–48 *(Left Monterey Turn)*	
	Waltz Steps with Quarter Turn	
61	Step left foot forward	
62	Step right foot next to left	
63	Step left foot in place	
64	Step right foot forward, making quarter turn to right	
65	Step left foot next to right	
66	Step right foot in place	
67	Step left foot forward, making quarter turn to right	
68	Step right foot next to left	
69	Step left foot next to right	
70–72	Repeat steps 64–66	
	Begin again!	

☆☆☆☆ The Dizzy Cowpoke ☆☆☆☆

Michael W. Diven *Two Wall*

This may be danced in opposing lines.

Beats	Movement	Direction
	Rock Steps and Pivot Turn	
1	Rock right foot forward	○
2	Rock back onto left foot	
3	Rock back onto right foot	
4	Rock forward onto left foot	
5	Step right foot forward	
6	Pivot half turn left	
7–12	Repeat steps 1–6	
	Right Vine	
13	Step right foot to right side	⇨
14	Step left foot behind right	
15	Step right foot to right side	
16	Stomp left foot beside right	
	Left Vine	
17	Step left foot to left side	⇦
18	Step right foot behind left	
19	Step left foot to left side	
20	Stomp right foot beside left	

(Contd.)

Beats	Movement	Direction
	Half Turns Rolling Forward	
21	Step right foot forward	
22	Turn half turn right on right foot stepping left foot back	◗
23	Turn half turn right on left foot stepping right foot forward	◗
24	Turn half turn right on right foot stepping left foot back	◗
	Walk Back, Drag Forward	
25	Step right foot back	⇩
26	Step left foot back	
27	Step right foot back	
28	Touch left toe back	
29	Step left foot forward	⇧
30	Slide right foot beside left	
31	Step left foot forward	
32	Scuff right foot forward	

Begin again!

☆☆☆☆☆☆☆☆☆ *Elvira* ☆☆☆☆☆☆☆☆☆

One Wall

Beats	Movement	Direction
	Shuffle Right and Rock	
1	Step right foot to right side	⇨
&	Step left foot beside right	
2	Step right foot to right side	
3	Rock back onto left foot	
4	Rock forward onto right foot	
	Shuffle Left and Rock	
5	Step left foot to left side	⇦
&	Step right foot beside left	
6	Step left foot to left side	
7	Rock back onto right foot	
8	Rock forward onto left foot	
	Shuffle, Half Turn, Shuffle, Quarter Turn	
9&10	Shuffle forward, right, left, right	⇧
11	Step left foot forward	
12	Pivot half turn right	◗
13&14	Shuffle forward, left, right, left	⇧
15	Step right foot forward	
16	Pivot quarter turn left	◖

(Contd.)

Beats	Movement	Direction
	Half Turn, Shuffle, Half Turn, Shuffle	
17	Step right foot forward	
18	Pivot half turn left	
19&20	Shuffle forward, right, left, right	
21	Step left foot forward	
22	Pivot half turn right	
23&24	Shuffle forward, left, right, left	
	Walk Forward, Kick	
25	Step right foot forward, turning quarter turn to left	
26	Step left foot forward	
27	Step right foot forward	
28	Kick left foot forward, clap	
	Walk Backward, Stomp	
29	Step left foot back	
30	Step right foot back	
31	Step left foot back	
32	Stomp right foot beside left *(with no weight on stomp*	

Begin again!

☆☆☆☆☆ Emilio Shuffle ☆☆☆☆☆

Barry W. Muniz, Danville, USA — ***Four Wall***

Beats	Movement	Direction
	Shuffle-steps with Turns	
1&2	Left shuffle-step forward *(left, right, left in two beats)*	⇧
3&4	Right shuffle-step forward, making quarter turn to right on first step *(step right with quarter turn, step left, step right in two beats)*	◗
5&6	Left shuffle-step forward *(left, right, left)*	⇧
7&8	Right shuffle-step forward, making a quarter turn to right on first step	◗
	Double Hitch	
9–10	Hitch *(raise)* left knee twice	❍
	Coaster Step	
11	Step left foot slightly back	❍
&	Step right foot next to left	
12	Step left foot slightly forward	
	Double Hitch	
13–14	Hitch right knee twice	❍

(Contd.)

Beats	Movement	Direction
	Coaster Step	
15	Step right foot slightly back	❍
&	Step left foot next to right	
16	Step right foot slightly forward	
	Cross Over	
17	Touch left toe over and in front of right	❍
18	Touch left toe out to left side	
19	Touch left toe over and in front of right	
20	Touch left toe out to left side	
	Side-shuffle	
21&22	Shuffle-step to left, while facing forward *(left, right, left)*	⇦
23&24	Shuffle-step to right, while facing forward *(right, left, right)* and making quarter turn to right with last step	⇨ ◗
25	Touch left heel forward with toe pointed in	❍
26	Swivel left toe out to left	
27	Step left foot next to right	
&	Step right in place	
28	Step left in place	
29	Kick right foot out to right side	❍
30	Cross right foot behind left	

Beats	Movement	Direction
31	Make half turn to right, unwinding legs	◗
32	Hold and clap	
	Cross Kick	
33	Hook left ankle in front of right shin, left knee bent	❍
34	Kick left foot forward	
	Shuffle-step Back	
35&36	Left shuffle-step backward *(left, right, left)*	⇩
	Cross Kick	
37	Hook right ankle in front of left shin, right knee bent	❍
38	Kick right foot forward	
39&40	Right shuffle-step backward *(right, left, right)*	⇩
	Begin again!	

☆☆☆☆☆☆ Firecracker ☆☆☆☆☆☆

Yvonne Gonzalez **Four Wall**

Take it easy on the jumps in this dance. You can land gently on one foot and then the other in the space of one beat.

Beats	Movement	Direction
	Step and Touch	
1	Step left foot forward	❍
2	Touch right heel forward	
3	Step right foot back	
4	Touch left toe back	
5–8	Repeat steps 1–4	
	Weave	
9	Step left foot to left	⇦
10	Cross right foot behind left	
11	Step left foot to left	
12	Cross right foot over left	
13	Step left foot to left	
14	Cross right foot behind left	
15	Step left foot to left	
16	Stomp right foot next to left	
	Turning Step-hitches	
17	Step right foot to right, making	◗

Beats	Movement	Direction
	quarter turn to right	
18	Hitch left knee (lift up)	
19	Step left foot to left, making quarter turn to left	
20	Hitch right knee	
21–24	Repeat steps 17–20	
	Jumps	
25	Jump forward on both feet	⇧
26	Hold and clap	
27	Jump back on both feet	⇩
28	Hold and clap	
	Shuffle-step with Quarter Turn	
29	Step right foot forward, turning foot slightly to right	
&	Slide left foot up to meet right	
30	Step right foot in place, completing quarter turn to right	
	Shuffle-step with Half Turn	
31	Step left foot forward, turning foot slightly to left	
&	Slide right foot around to right of left foot	
32	Step left foot to left, finishing half turn	

(Contd.)

Beats	Movement	Direction
	Struts	
33	Touch right toe forward	⇧
34	Lower right heel	
35	Touch left toe forward	
36	Lower left heel	
	Kick and Turn	
37	Kick right foot forward	❍
38	Cross right foot in front of left leg	
39	Pivot half turn to left on ball of left foot *(unwind legs)*	◖
40	Hold	
41–48	Repeat steps 33–40	
	Begin again!	

☆ Foot Boogie (a.k.a. Night Fever) ☆

Ryan Dobry, Nashville, USA — ***Two Wall***

This may be danced in opposing lines.

Beats	Movement	Direction
	Right Fan, Twice	
1	Fan right toes right	❍
2	Fan right toes centre	
3,4	Repeat steps 1,2	
	Left Fan, Twice	
5	Fan left toes left	❍
6	Fan left toes centre	
7,8	Repeat steps 5,6	
	Right Toe, Heel, Heel, Toe	
9	Fan right toes right	❍
10	Swing right heel right	
11	Swing right heel left	
12	Fan right toes centre	
	Left Toe, Heel, Heel, Toe	
13	Fan left toes left	❍
14	Swing left heel left	
15	Swing left heel right	
16	Fan left toes centre	

(Contd.)

Beats	Movement	Direction
	Both Feet, Toe, Heel, Heel, Toe	
17	Fan both feet out	○
18	Swing both heels out	
19	Swing both heels in	
20	Fan both feet centre	
	Step, Slide, Step, Hitch	
21	Step right foot forward	⇧
22	Slide left foot to meet right	
23	Step right foot forward	
24	Hitch left *(raise knee)*	
	Step, Slide, Step, Turn	
25	Step left foot forward	⇧
26	Slide right foot to meet left	
27	Step left foot forward	
28	Pivot half turn left with right knee hitched	◖
	Step, Slide, Step, Slide	
29	Step right foot forward	⇧
30	Slide left foot to meet right	
31	Step right foot forward	
32	Slide left foot to meet right	

Begin again!

☆☆☆☆☆ Four Star Boogie ☆☆☆☆☆

Melanie Greenwood, USA | | ***Four Wall***

Beats	Movement	Direction
	Syncopated Jumps	
&1	Jump forward onto right foot, then left foot beside right	⇧
2	Clap	
&3	Jump backward onto left foot, then right foot beside left	⇩
4	Clap	
	Side Shuffle Right and Left	
5&6	Shuffle to right side *(right, left, right)*	⇨
7&8	Shuffle to left side *(left, right, left)*	⇦
	Side Shuffle Right, Half Turn, Side Shuffle Left	
9&10	Shuffle to right side *(right, left, right)* half turn right	⇨ ◗
11&12	Shuffle to left side *(left, right, left)*	⇦
	Right Vine with Half Turn Right	
13	Step right foot to right side	⇨

(Contd.)

Beats	Movement	Direction
14	Step left foot behind right	
15	Step right foot forward, turning quarter turn right	◝
16	Step left foot beside right, turning another quarter turn right	◝
	Right Kick-Ball-Change, Twice	
17	Kick right foot forward	○
&	Step on ball of right foot	
18	Step left foot beside right	
19&20	Repeat steps 17&18	
	Quarter Turn Left, Left Kick-Ball-Change	
21	Step right foot forward, turning quarter turn left	◜
22	Kick left foot forward	○
&	Step on ball of left foot	
23	Step right foot beside left	
24	Step left foot beside right, clap	
	Shuffle Forward and Half Turn Right	
25&26	Shuffle forward right, left, right	⇧
27	Step left foot forward	
28	Pivot half turn right	◗

Beats	Movement	Direction
	Star Jump (Syncopated)	
29	Point left toe to left side	❍
&	Jump left foot back to centre	
30	Point right toe to right side	
&	Jump right foot to centre, making half turn left	◖
31	Tap left heel forward	
&	Jump left foot to centre	❍
32	Tap right toe back	

Begin again!

☆☆☆☆☆☆ Good Ol' Boys ☆☆☆☆☆☆

Four Wall

Beats	Movement	Direction
	Heel Splits	
1	Swing heels out	❍
2	Swing heels in	
3,4	Repeat steps 1,2	
	Hitches and Touches	
5	Hitch right leg up *(raise knee)*	❍
6	Step right foot in place	
7	Touch left toe back	
8	Step left foot in place	
9–12	Repeat steps 5–8	
	Heel Digs	
13	Tap right heel forward	❍
14	Step right foot in place	
15	Tap left heel forward	
16	Step left foot in place	
17–20	Repeat steps 13–16	
	Toe Touches and Quarter Turn	
21	Forward *(Touching right toe)*	❍
22	To right side	
23	Behind	

Beats	Movement	Direction
24	To right side	❍
25	Behind	
26	Hook behind left ankle, quarter turn left	◖
	Right Vine and Scuff	
27	Step right foot to right side	⇨
28	Step left foot behind right	
29	Step right foot to right side	
30	Scuff left foot forward	
	Left Vine and Scuff	
31	Step left foot to left side	⇦
32	Step right foot behind left	
33	Step left foot to left side	
34	Scuff right foot forward	
	Walk Back	
35	Step right foot back	⇩
36	Step left foot back	
37	Step right foot back	
38	Scuff left foot forward	
	Step Forward and Stomp	
39	Step left foot forward	⇧
40	Stomp right foot behind left	
41–46	Repeat steps 39,40 three times more	
	Begin again!	

☆☆☆☆☆☆ The Grundy ☆☆☆☆☆☆

Tom Via, Richmond, USA — ***One Wall***

Beats	Movement	Direction
	Kick-Ball-Touch	
1	Kick right foot forward	○
&	Step right foot next to left	
2	Touch left toe out to left side	
3	Kick left foot forward	
&	Step left foot next to right	
4	Touch right toe out to right side	
	Right Side Steps	
5	Step right foot to right and dip right shoulder	⇨
&	Step left foot next to right	
6	Step right foot to right and dip right shoulder	
&	Step left foot next to right	
7	Step right foot to right and dip right shoulder	
&	Step left foot next to right	
8	Step right foot to right and dip right shoulder	
	Kick-Ball-Touch	
9	Kick left foot forward	

Beats	Movement	Direction
&	Step left foot next to right	○
10	Touch right toe out to right side	
11	Kick right foot forward	
&	Step right foot next to left	
12	Touch left toe out to left side	
	Left Side Steps	
13–16	Repeat steps 5–8 to the left	⇦
	Kick-Ball-Change	
17	Kick right foot forward	○
&	Step right foot next to left	
18	Step left foot next to right *(in place)*	
19	Stomp right foot	
20	Stomp left foot	
	Backward Skips	
21–24	Skip backward, right, left, right, left, swinging opposite leg out to side	⇩
	Shuffle-steps	
25&26	Right shuffle-step forward *(right, left, right)*	⇧
27&28	Left shuffle-step forward *(left, right, left)*	

(Contd.)

Beats	Movement	Direction
	Half Turn	
29	Step right foot forward	◖
30	Make half turn to left, switching weight to left foot	
	Shuffle-steps	
31–34	Repeat steps 25–28	⇧
	Stomps	
35	Stomp right foot next to left	❍
36	Stomp left foot in place	
	Foot Twists (Apple Jack)	
	This move may take a little practice, so break it down and do it slowly until you can get up to speed	
37	With weight on left heel and right toe, swivel left toe and right heel to left	❍
&	Swivel toe and heel back to centre, switch weight to left toe and right heel	
38	Swivel left heel and right toe to right	
&	Swivel heel and toe back to centre and switch weight to left heel and right toe	

Beats	Movement	Direction
39	Swivel left toe and right heel to left	❍
&	Swivel toe and heel back to centre, switch weight to left toe and right heel	
40	Swivel left heel and right toe to right	
&	Swivel heel and toe back to centre	

Begin again!

☆☆☆☆ *Hawaiian Hustle* ☆☆☆☆

Sue Shotwell, USA — ***Two Wall***

Beats	Movement	Direction
	Toe, Touch, Chassé Right	
1,2	Touch right toe forward. Touch right toe beside left	❍
3,4	Step right foot to right side. Slide left foot to meet right	⇨
5–8	Repeat steps 3,4 twice	

Beats	Movement	Direction
	Toe, Touch, Heel, Touch, Bump Hips	
9,10	Touch left toe to left side. Touch left toe beside right foot	❍
11,12	Touch left heel forward. Touch left foot beside right	
13	Step left foot back diagonally left bumping hips to left *(elbows to side, forearm extended forward parallel to ground, clenched fists turned upward)*	⇗
14	Bump hips forward diagonally right *(pull fists and forearms up to right shoulder)*	
15	Bump hips back diagonally left *(arms bent, fists clenched as before)*	❍
16	Bump hips forward diagonally right *(pull fists back)*	

Beats	Movement	Direction
	Left Vine with Half Turn, Vine, Cross Feet	
17,18	Step left foot to left side. Step right foot behind left	⇦
19,20	Step left foot to left side. Pivot half turn left on ball of left foot, raise right knee	◖
21,22	Step right foot to right side. Step left foot behind right	⇨
23,24	Step right foot to right side. Cross left foot over right	
	Toe, Together, Toe, Together, Swivel Heels	
25,26	Touch right toe to right side. Step right foot beside left	○
27,28	Touch left toe to left side. Step left foot beside right	
29	Pivot on balls of feet swinging heels 1/8 turn right	
30	Pivot on balls of feet swinging heels back to centre	
31	Pivot on balls of feet swinging heels 1/8 turn left	
32	Pivot on balls of feet swinging heels back to centre	

(Contd.)

Beats	Movement	Direction
	Kick-Ball-Change, Half Turn, Hold (x2)	
33–36	Right kick-ball-change twice	❍
37	Cross right foot over left	
38	Unwind half turn left on balls of both feet	◖
39	Drop heels to floor	
40	Hold	
41–48	Repeat steps 33–40	
	Knee Pops	
49	Right foot in place, raise right heel	❍
50	Right foot in place, lower heel to floor	
51	Left foot in place, raise left heel	
52	Left foot in place, lower heel to floor	
	(Motion resembles climbing down and back up an imaginary ladder.)	
53	Step right foot in place, start bending knees	❍
54	Step left foot in place, knees bent	
55	Step right foot in place, start straightening knees	
56	Step left foot in place, knees straight	

Beats	Movement	Direction
	'Hula Wiggle'	
57	Step right foot to right side, hips wiggle in hula motion, arms do wave motion	⇨
58	Slide left foot to right, continuing 'hula wiggle'	
59,60	Repeat steps 57,58	
61	Step left foot to left side . . . 'hula wiggle'	⇦
62	Slide right foot to meet left . . . 'hula wiggle'	
63,64	Repeat steps 61,62	

Begin again!

☆☆☆☆☆☆☆ Hit Kick ☆☆☆☆☆☆☆

Kevin Richards, South Glen Falls, USA — ***One Wall***

Beats	Movement	Direction
	Walk Forward and Kicks	
1	Step right foot forward	⇧
2	Step left foot forward	
3–4	Kick right foot forward twice	❍
	Walk Back and Kicks	
5	Step right foot back	⇩
6	Step left foot back	
7–8	Kick right foot back twice	❍
	Scuff Kick	
9	Scuff right foot forward	❍
10	Step right foot over left	
11–12	Kick left foot out to left twice	
	Jazz Box	
13	Step left foot across right foot	❍
14	Step right foot back	
15	Step left foot next to right	
16	Step right foot in place	
	Snap and Twist	
17–18	Bend knees, snap fingers twice to right	❍

Beats	Movement	Direction
19–20	With knees still bent, snap fingers twice to left	○
	Crossfire	
21	Straightening legs, scuff right foot forward	○
22	Step right foot in place	
23	Step left foot across right foot	
24	Touch right toe to right side	
25	Stomp right foot	○
26	Hold	
27&28	Stomp right foot three times	
29	With weight on left foot, push off on toes of right foot . . .	
30	. . . and make quarter turn to left	◢
31	With weight on left foot, push off on toes of right foot . . .	
32	. . . and make quarter turn to left	◢
33–44	Repeat steps 21–32	
45	Scuff right foot	○
46	Step right foot to right	
47	Scuff left foot	
48	Step left foot to left	

(Contd.)

Beats	Movement	Direction
	Hip Bumps	
49	Bump hips to left and slap left hip	❍
50	Bump hips to right and slap right hip	
51&52	Bump hips left, right, left	
	Hand Jive	
53–54	Pass right hand over left while bumping hips to left twice	❍
55	Slap right hand up and left hand down and bump hips to right	
56	Slap right hand down and left hand up and bump hips to left	

Begin again!

☆☆☆☆☆☆☆ Hold Up! ☆☆☆☆☆☆☆

Joe White, Milmont Park, USA | ***Four Wall***

Beats	Movement	Direction
	Stomp and Hold	
1	Stomp right foot forward	⇧
2	Hold *(switch weight to right foot)*	
3	Stomp left foot forward	
4	Hold	
	Step Swivels	
5	Step right foot forward	⇧
&	Swivel right heel to right, left heel lifted slightly	
6	Step left foot forward	
&	Swivel left heel to left, right heel lifted slightly	
7&	Repeat step 5&	
8&	Repeat step 6&	
9	Tap right heel forward	❍
10	Hold	
11&12	Shuffle-step in place: step right foot, step left foot, stomp right foot	
13	Tap left heel forward	
14	Hold	
15&16	Shuffle-step in place: step left foot, step right foot, stomp left foot	

(Contd.)

Beats	Movement	Direction
	Shuffle and Pivot	
17&18	Right shuffle-step forward (right, left, right)	⇧
19	Step left foot forward	
20	Make half turn to right *(keep weight on left foot)*	◗
	Shuffle and Pivot	
21&22	Left shuffle-step forward (left, right, left)	⇧
23	Step right foot forward	
24	Make half turn to left *(now facing original wall, keep weight on right foot)*	◖
	Reverse Vine Left	
25	Cross step right foot in front of left	⇦
26	Hold	
27	Step left foot to left side	
28	Hold	
29	Cross step right foot in front of left	
30	Step left foot to left	
31	Cross step right foot in front of left	
32	Touch left toe to left	
	Reverse Vine Right	
33	Cross step left foot in front of right	⇨

Beats	Movement	Direction
34	Hold	
35	Step right foot to right side	⇨
36	Hold	
37	Cross step left foot in front of right	
38	Step right foot to right side	
39	Cross step left foot in front of right	
40	Touch right toe to right side	
	Scuffs and Turn	
41	Scuff right foot forward	○
42	Scuff right foot back, making quarter turn to left	◔
43	Stomp right foot *(switch weight to right foot)*	○
44	Stomp left foot *(switch weight to left foot)*	

Begin again!

☆☆☆☆ Howlin' at Midnight ☆☆☆☆

Nancy DeMoss, Danville, USA — ***Four Wall***

Beats	Movement	Direction
	Boogie Moves	
1–2	With weight on left foot, roll right knee clockwise	❍
3–4	With weight on right foot, roll left knee counterclockwise	
5–8	Repeat steps 1–4	
	Vine with Jump and Hip Rolls	
9	Step right foot to right	⇨
10	Cross left foot behind right	
11	Jump right foot to right side, setting left heel forward	
12	Jump, bringing both feet together	
13–16	Two hip rolls clockwise, two beats each	❍
	Vine with Jump	
17	Step left foot to left side	⇦
18	Cross right foot behind left	
19	Jump left foot to left, setting right heel forward	
20	Jump, bringing feet together	
21–24	Two hip rolls counterclockwise, two beats each	❍

Beats	Movement	Direction
	Toe Struts and Kick-Ball-Changes	
25	Small step forward on ball of right foot	⇧
26	Bring heel down while snapping fingers	
27	Small step forward on ball of left foot	
28	Bring heel down while snapping fingers	
29	Kick right foot forward	❍
&	Step on ball of right foot slightly behind left	
30	Step left foot next to right	
31&32	Repeat steps 29&30	
33–40	Repeat steps 25–32	
	Side Touches	
41	Touch right toe to right	❍
42	Step right foot next to left	
43	Touch left toe to left	
44	Step left foot next to right	
	Turn and Scoot	
45	Step right foot forward	
46	Make quarter turn to left	◀
47–48	Bringing right foot next to left, scoot	

(Contd.)

Beats	Movement	Direction
	forward twice with feet together	⇧
49–56	Repeat steps 41–48	
	Hip Rolls	
57–58	Roll hips counterclockwise, two beats, turning slightly to left	
59–64	Repeat steps 57–58 three times, completing half turn to left	◖
	Begin again!	

☆☆☆☆☆☆ *Interchange* ☆☆☆☆☆☆

Four Wall

Beats	**Movement**	**Direction**
	Touch Right, Left, Right, Hold (Syncopated)	
1	Touch right foot to right side	○
&	Jump right foot back to centre	
2	Touch left foot to left side	
&	Jump left foot back to centre	
3	Touch right foot to right side	
4	Hold	
	Touch Left, Right, Left, Hold	
&	Jump right foot back to centre	○
5	Touch left foot to left side	
&	Jump left foot back to centre	
6	Touch right foot to right side	
&	Jump right foot back to centre	
7	Touch left foot to left side	
8	Hold	
	Pivot Turn and Stomp	
9	Step left foot forward	
10	Pivot quarter turn right	◗
11	Stomp right foot in place	○
12	Stomp left foot in place	

(Contd.)

Beats	Movement	Direction
	Kick-Ball-Change, Step and Touch	
13	Kick right foot forward	❍
&	Step on ball of right foot	
14	Step left foot in place	
15&16	Repeat steps 13&14	
17	Step right foot forward	⇧
18	Touch left foot beside right	
19	Kick left foot forward	❍
&	Step on ball of left foot	
20	Step right foot in place	
21&22	Repeat steps 19&20	
23	Step left foot back	⇩
24	Touch right foot beside left	
	Heel Hooks	
25	Tap right heel forward	❍
26	Hook right foot over left shin	
27	Tap right heel forward	
28	Step right foot beside left	
29	Tap left heel forward	❍
30	Hook left foot over right shin	
31	Tap left heel forward	
32	Step left foot beside right	

Beats	Movement	Direction
	Monterey Turns	
33	Touch right foot to right side	
34	Make half turn to right (swing right leg around) and step right foot beside left	◗
35	Touch left toe to left side	
36	Step left foot beside right	
38–40	Repeat steps 33–36	

Begin again!

☆☆☆☆☆☆ The J Walk ☆☆☆☆☆☆

Sue Lipscomb, Chicago, USA — ***Four Wall***

Beats	Movement	Direction
1	Rock forward on right heel	○
2	Rock back onto left foot	
3&4	Triple-step in place (right, left, right)	
5	Rock forward on left heel	○
6	Rock back onto right foot	
7&8	Triple-step in place (left, right, left)	
9	Step right foot forward	
10	Make quarter turn to left, switching weight to ball of left foot	◖
11	Stomp right foot next to left and transfer weight to right	○
12	Stomp left foot next to right and transfer weight to left	
13	Push right knee out in front	○
14	Hold	
15	Bring right knee in and push left knee out in front *(keep left heel on floor and weight on left foot)*	
16	Hold	

Beats	Movement	Direction
	Walk Forward	
17	Step right foot forward	⇧
18	Step left foot forward	
19	Step right foot forward	
20	Make half turn to left on balls of feet, keeping weight on right foot	◖
	Hitchhike Back	
	Hand movements: Hitch right thumb over shoulder with each step	
21	Step left foot back	⇩
22	Step right foot back	
23	Step left foot back	
24	Touch right toes beside left	
	Strut Forward	
25	Touch right toes out to right side	⇧
26	Step right foot across left	
27	Touch left toes out to left side	
28	Step left foot across right	
29	Touch right toes out to right side	
30	Step right foot across left	
31	Make half turn to left, unwinding legs	◖
32	Clap and end with weight on left foot	

Begin again!

☆☆☆☆☆ Jo T. Jam ☆☆☆☆☆

Jo Thompson, Nashville, USA — ***Four Wall***

Beats	Movement	Direction
	Step, Touch Right and Left	
1,2	Step right foot to right side. Touch left foot beside right	❍
3,4	Step left foot to left side. Touch right foot beside left	
5–8	Repeat steps 1–4	
	Funky Heel Lifts	
9	Lift left heel and flex knee in front of right and heel down	❍
10	Lift right heel and flex knee in front of left and heel down	
11	Lift left heel and flex knee in front of right and heel down	
12	Lift left heel and flex knee in front of right and heel down	
13	Lift right heel and flex knee in front of left and heel down	
14	Lift left heel and flex knee in front of right and heel down	
15	Lift right heel and flex knee in front of left and heel down	
16	Lift right heel and flex knee in front of left	

Beats	Movement	Direction
	Right Vine, Cross Kick	
17,18	Step right foot to right side. Step left foot behind right	⇨
19,20	Step right foot to right side. Kick left foot across right	
	Travelling Pigeon Toes Left	
21	Fan left toe out, right heel in	⇦
22	Shift weight to left toe and right heel. Fan left heel out and right toe in	
23	Shift weight to left heel and right toe. Fan left toe out and right heel in	
24	Shift weight to left toe and right heel. Fan left heel out and right toe in	
25–32	Repeat steps 17–24	
	Cross, Unwind, Scoot	
33,34	Cross right foot over left. Unwind half turn left	◖
35,36	Scoot forward on both feet	⇧
37–40	Repeat steps 33–36	
	Heel Shifts	
41&42	Touch right heel forward, switch left heel forward	○
&43,44	Switch right heel forward, tap twice	
&45	Touch left heel forward, switch right	

(Contd.)

Beats	Movement	Direction
&46	heel forward	❍
&47,48	Switch left heel forward, tap twice	
	Electric Stomps	
49,50	Step left foot forward. Stomp right foot beside left	❍
51,52	Step right foot back. Stomp left foot beside right	
53–56	Repeat steps 49–50	
	Pony L, R, L, R	
57	Slide left foot forward and pop right knee forward	⇧
58	Slide right foot forward and pop left knee forward	
59,60	Repeat steps 57,58	
	Quarter Turn, Hip Roll	
61,62	Step on left foot, turning quarter turn left. Step right foot beside left	◀
63,64	Circle hips counter-clockwise twice	❍

Begin again!

☆☆☆☆☆ José Cuervo '97 ☆☆☆☆☆

Max Perry, Danbury, USA **_Four Wall_**

Beats	Movement	Direction
	Dance begins with vocals . . . 1st verse	
	Side Steps, Sailor Shuffle	
1,2	Cross left foot over right. Step right foot to right side	⇨
3	Step left foot behind right	
&	Step right foot to right side	
4	Step left foot in place *(weight on right, feet slightly apart)*	
5,6	Cross right foot across left. Step left foot to left side	⇦
7	Step right foot behind left	
&	Step left foot to left side	
8	Step right foot in place *(weight on right foot, feet slightly apart)*	

Beats	Movement	Direction
	Weave and Turns	
9	Cross left foot over right	⇨
10	Step right foot to right side	
11	Step left foot behind right	
12	Step right foot forward, turning quarter turn right	◗
13	Step left foot forward	
14	Pivot half turn right, shift weight to right	◗

(Contd.)

Beats	Movement	Direction
15&16	Shuffle in place, left, right, left, turning one full turn right *(360 degrees clockwise)* *(Optional: shuffle in place without turn)*	●
	Walk, Kick-Ball-Change	
17,18	Step right foot forward. Step left forward	⇧
19	Kick right foot forward	○
&	Step right beside left on ball of foot	
20	Step left foot beside right	
21&22	Repeat steps 19&20	
23,24	Step right foot forward. Step left foot forward	⇧
	Monterey, Shuffle	
25	Touch right toe to right side	
26	Pivot half turn right on ball of right foot. Step left foot beside right on completion of turn	◗
27,28	Touch left toe to left side. Step left foot beside right	
29&30	Shuffle to right side, right, left, right	⇨
31,32	Stomp left foot beside right. Kick left foot forward.	

Begin again!

☆☆☆☆☆☆ Just for Grins ☆☆☆☆☆☆

Jo Thompson, Nashville, USA **Four Wall**

Beats	Movement	Direction
	Kick-Ball-Change, Stomp, Clap	
1	Kick right foot forward	⇧
&	Step on ball of right foot	
2	Step left foot in place	
3,4	Stomp right foot forward, Clap	
5	Kick left foot forward	⇧
&	Step on ball of left foot	
6	Step right foot in place	
7,8	Stomp left foot forward. Clap	
	Touch Forward, Side, Change Touch, Change Touch	
9	Touch right toe forward	❍
10	Touch right toe to right side	
&	Step on ball of right foot *(in place)*	
11	Touch left toe to left side	
&	Stomp on ball of left foot *(in place)*	
12	Touch right toe to right side	
13–16	Repeat steps 9–12	

(Contd.)

Beats	Movement	Direction
	Right Vine, Touch, Bump Hips	
17	Step right foot to right side	⇨
18	Step left foot behind right	
19	Step right foot to right side	
20	Touch left foot beside right	
21	Step left foot to left side, bumping hips left	❍
22–24	Bump hips right, left, right	
	Left Vine, Touch, Bump Hips	
25	Step left foot to left side	⇦
26	Step right foot behind left	
27	Step left foot to left side	
28	Touch right foot beside left	
29	Step right foot to right side bumping hips right	❍
30–32	Bump hips left, right, left *(Variation for bump hips: hip rolls, double bumps, body rolls, etc.)*	
	Figure-eight Right Vine	
33	Step right foot to right side	⇨
34	Step left foot behind right	
35	Step right foot to right side, turning quarter turn right	◗
36	Step left foot forward	
37	Pivot half turn right	◗

Beats	Movement	Direction
	(shifting weight to right foot)	
38	Step left foot to left side, turning slightly to face original wall *(12 o'clock)*	⇦
39	Step right foot behind left	
40	Step left foot to left side, turning quarter turn left *(Now facing 9 o'clock)*	◖

Shuffle Forward, Pivot Turn

Beats	Movement	Direction
41&42	Shuffle forward right, left, right	⇧
43	Step left foot forward	
44	Pivot half turn right	◗
45&46	Shuffle forward left, right, left	⇧
47	Step right foot forward	
48	Pivot half turn left	◖

Begin again!

☆☆☆☆☆ Kelly's Cannibals ☆☆☆☆☆

Liz and Bev Clarke, UK

Two Wall

Beats	Movement	Direction
	Toe Struts	
1	Touch right toe forward	⇧
2	Slap right heel down	
3	Touch left toe forward	
4	Slap left heel down	
5–8	Repeat steps 1–4	
	Hip Bumps	
9	Bump hips right	○
10	Hold	
11	Bump hips left	
12	Hold	
13–16	Bump hips, right, left, right, left	
	Jazz Box with Quarter Turn	
17	Cross right foot over left	
18	Step left foot back	◗
19	Step right foot, turning quarter turn right	
20	Step left foot beside right	
21–24	Repeat steps 17–20	
	Kick and Triple-step	
25,26	Kick right foot forward twice	○

Beats	Movement	Direction
27&28	Step right, left, right in place	◯
29,30	Kick left foot forward twice	
31&32	Step left, right, left in place	
	Monterey Turn	
33	Touch right toe to right side	
34	Make half turn to right *(swing right leg around)* and step right foot beside left	◗
35	Touch left toe to left side	
36	Step left foot beside right	
37–40	Repeat steps 33–36	
	Begin again!	

☆☆☆☆☆ Kickin' Country ☆☆☆☆☆

Stella Cabeca, North Miami Beach, USA — ***Two Wall***

Beats	Movement	Direction
	Right Kick-Ball-Change	
1	Kick right foot forward	❍
&	Step on ball of right foot next to left foot	
2	Change weight to left foot	
3&4	Kick right foot forward, step on ball of right, change weight to left foot	
5	Kick right foot forward	❍
6	Step right foot back	
7	Step left foot forward	
8	Step right foot next to left	

Beats	Movement	Direction
	Left Kick-Ball-Change	
9	Kick left foot forward	❍
&	Step on ball of left foot next to right	
10	Change weight to right foot	
11&12	Kick left foot forward, step on ball of left foot, change weight to right foot	
13	Kick left foot forward	❍
14	Step left foot back	
15	Step right foot forward	
16	Step left foot next to right	

Beats	Movement	Direction
	Side Touches	
17	Step left foot to left	○
18	Touch right foot next to left	
19	Step right foot to right	
20	Touch left foot next to right	
	Left Turning Vine	
21	Step left foot to left, making quarter turn to left	⇦ ◀
22	Step right foot around left, making quarter turn to left	◀
23	Pivot half turn on ball of right foot, stepping left foot to left	◖
24	Touch right foot next to left	
	Side Touches	
25	Step right foot to right	○
26	Touch left foot next to right	
27	Step left foot to left	
28	Touch right foot next to left	
	Right Turning Vine	
29	Step right foot to right, making quarter turn to right	⇨ ▶
30	Step left foot around right, making quarter turn to right	▶
31	Pivot half turn on ball of left foot, stepping right foot to right	◗

(Contd.)

Beats	Movement	Direction
32	Touch left foot next to right	❍
33	Step left foot to left	
&	Step right foot next to left	
34	Step left foot to left	
35–36	Kick right foot across left leg twice	
37	Step right foot to right	❍
&	Step left foot next to right	
38	Step right foot to right	
39–40	Kick left foot across right leg twice	
41	Hop back onto left foot and touch right heel forward	
42	Hold	
43	Hop back onto right foot and touch left heel forward	⇩
44	Hold	
45	Jump both feet apart	❍
46	Jump, landing right foot across left	
47	Unwind legs, making half turn to left	◖
48	Hold and clap	

Begin again!

☆☆☆☆☆☆ L. A. Walk ☆☆☆☆☆☆

Four Wall

Beats	Movement	Direction
1	Touch right foot out to right	❍
2	Bring back next to left	
3	Touch right foot out to right	
4	Bring back next to left	
5	Touch left foot out to left	
6	Bring back next to right	
7	Touch left foot out to left	
8	Bring back next to right	

Heel Taps

Beats	Movement	Direction
9,10	Tap right heel forward twice	❍
11,12	Tap right toe back twice	
13	Tap right heel forward once	
14	Tap right toe back once	

Pivot Turns

Beats	Movement	Direction
15	Touch right foot forward	
16	Pivot half turn left *(keeping weight on left foot)*	◖
17	Touch right foot forward	
18	Pivot half turn left *(keeping weight on left foot)*	◖

(Contd.)

Beats	Movement	Direction
19	Touch right heel forward once	❍
20	Touch right toe back once	
21	Step forward on right, turning a quarter turn to right	◗
22	Touch left toe out to left side	
23	Cross left foot over right	
24	Touch right foot out to right side	
	Jazz Box	
25	Cross right foot over left	❍
26	Step back on left foot	
27	Step to right with right foot	
28	Step left next to right	

Begin again!

☆☆☆☆☆ Las Vegas Strut ☆☆☆☆☆

Four Wall

Beats	Movement	Direction
1	Tap right heel forward	❍
2	Hook right foot over left shin	
3	Tap right heel forward	
4	Kick right foot out to right side	
5	Tap right heel forward	
6	Step right foot beside left	
	Repeat steps 1–6 on left foot	
7	Tap left heel forward	❍
8	Hook left foot over right shin	
9	Tap left heel forward	
10	Kick left foot out to left side	
11	Tap left heel forward	
12	Step left foot beside right	
	Charleston Step, Step Forward and Half Turn	
13	Step left foot forward	❍
14	Kick right foot forward	
15	Step right foot back	
16	Touch left toe behind	
17	Step left foot forward	

(Contd.)

Beats	Movement	Direction
18	Lock right foot behind left	⇧
19	Step left foot forward	
20	Pivot half turn left on left foot	◖
	Heel Struts	
21	Step right heel forward	⇧
22	Slap right foot down	
23	Step left heel forward	
24	Slap left foot down	
25–28	Repeat steps 21–24	
	Jazz Box with Quarter Turn Right	
29	Cross right foot over left	
30	Step left foot back	
31	Step right foot forward, turning quarter turn right	◔
32	Step left foot beside right	
	Jazz Box	
33	Cross right foot over left	❍
34	Step left foot back	
35	Step right foot to right side	
36	Step left foot beside right	

Begin again!

☆☆☆☆☆☆☆ *Linda Lu* ☆☆☆☆☆☆☆

Neil Hale, Pleasanton, USA — ***Two Wall***

Beats	Movement	Direction
	Toe Points and Cross-Ball-Changes	
1,2	Touch right toe forward. Touch right toe to right side	❍
3	Cross right foot behind left	
&	Step on ball of left foot in place	
4	Step right foot to right side *(weight on right)*	
5,6	Touch left toe forward. Touch left toe to left side	
7	Cross left foot behind right	
&	Step on ball of right foot in place	
8	Step left foot to left side *(weight on left)*	

Beats	Movement	Direction
	& Right Vine, & Left Vine	
&	Take a small step back on right foot	⇨
9,10	Cross left foot over right. Step right foot to right side	
11,12	Cross left foot behind right. Step right foot to right side	
&	Take a small step back on left foot	
13,14	Cross right foot over left. Step left foot to left side	⇦

(Contd.)

Beats	Movement	Direction
15,16	Cross right foot behind left. Step left foot to left side	⇦
	Out-Out, In-In Syncopation, Cross, Unwind	
&17	Right foot steps right side. Left foot steps left side	❍
18	Hold & Clap	
&19	Right foot steps centre. Left foot steps centre	
20	Hold & Clap	
21,22	Cross right foot over left bending knees. Unwind half turn left as you straighten up and rise to balls of feet	◖
23,24	Drop down onto heels. Hold & Clap	
	Out-Out, In-In Syncopation, Travelling Backwards	
&25–28	Repeat steps &17–20	❍
	Next 4 counts, travel backwards	
&29	Right foot small step back. Left foot small step back (Out-Out)	⇩
&30	Right foot step back and centre. Left foot step back and to centre (In-In)	
&31–32	Repeat steps &29–30 (end with weight on left)	

Beats	Movement	Direction
	'Wiggle Walks' Travelling Forward	
33	Step right foot into a quarter turn left, bumping hips right	◀
34	Hold & Clap	
35	Pivot quarter turn right on ball of right foot, touching left foot beside right	▶
36	Hold & Clap	
37	Step left foot into a quarter turn right, bumping hips left	▶
38	Hold & Clap	
39	Pivot quarter turn left on ball of left foot, touching right foot beside left	◀
40	Hold & Clap	
41–48	Repeat steps 33–40	

Begin again!

Max Perry, Danbury, USA — ***Four Wall***

Beats	Movement	Direction
	Hip Bumps and Cross Steps	
1	Step right foot forward, bump hips right	❍
2	Bump hips left	
3	Bump hips right	
4	Bump hips left	
5	Cross right foot behind left	⇦
6	Step left foot to left side	
7	Step right foot forward, taking weight	
8	Hold	
	Repeat steps 1–8 left foot leading . . .	
9	Step left foot forward, bump hips left	❍
10	Bump hips right	
11	Bump hips left	
12	Bump hips right	
13	Cross left foot behind right	⇨
14	Step right foot to right side	
15	Step left foot forward taking weight	
16	Hold	
	Half Turns	
17	Step right foot forward	⇧
18	Hold	

Beats	Movement	Direction
19	Pivot half turn left	◖
20	Hold	
21–24	Repeat steps 17–20	
	Right Vine with Quarter Turn	
25	Step right foot to right side	⇨
26	Step left foot behind right	
27	Step right foot forward turning quarter turn right	◗
28	Scuff left foot forward	
	360-degree Turn Left	
29	Step left foot forward	
30–32	Rotate 360 degrees left, swivel or hop on left foot with right knee hitched or right leg back slightly and arms out for balance *(as if playing 'aeroplanes')*	●
	Begin again!	

☆☆☆☆☆ Lonestar Shuffle ☆☆☆☆☆

Andie Lynne | **_Four Wall_**

Beats	Movement	Direction
	Jump and Walk	
1	Hold arms out in front	⇧
2	Hop forward while pulling arms in	
3	Step forward on right foot	
4	Step forward on left foot	
	Jazz Box	
5	Step right foot over left	❍
6	Step back on left foot	
7	Step back on right foot, to the right of left foot	
8	Step left foot next to right	
	Heel Taps	
9–10	Tap right heel forward twice	❍
&	Switch feet – step on right foot	
11–12	Tap left heel forward twice	
&13	Switch feet – step on left foot – and tap right heel forward once	
&14	Switch feet – step on right foot – and tap left heel forward once	
&15 –16	Switch feet – step on left foot – and tap right heel forward twice	

Beats	Movement	Direction
	Right Vine	
17	Step right foot to right	⇨
18	Cross left foot behind right	
19	Step right foot to right	
20	Hold and clap	
	Knee Swings	
21–22	Swing right knee to right and return	❍
23–24	Swing left knee to left and return	
	Left Vine	
25	Step left foot to left	⇦
26	Cross right foot behind left	
27	Step left foot to left	
28	Hold and clap	
	Knee Swings	
29–30	Swing right knee to right and return	❍
31–32	Swing left knee to left and return	
	Quarter Turn	
33	Sweep right foot forward	❍
34	Cross right foot over left	
35	Tap right toe in front of left foot	
36	Make quarter turn to left, staying on right toe	◖

(Contd.)

Beats	Movement	Direction
	Knee Pops	
37–40	Transfer weight to right foot, left foot, right foot, left foot – as if marching in place	❍

Begin again!

☆☆☆☆☆☆ Lost in Texas ☆☆☆☆☆☆

Jim Williams, Half Moon Bay, USA ***Four Wall***

Beats	Movement	Direction
	Charleston Stomps	
1	Step left foot forward	❍
2	Stomp right foot beside left	
3	Step right foot back	
4	Touch left foot beside right	
	Swivet	
	Weight on ball of left foot and heel of right	
5	Swivel right toe to right side and left heel to left side; hitch-hike right thumb	❍
6	Swivel right heel and left toe back to centre	
7,8	Repeat steps 5,6	
	Quarter Turn and Repeat Pattern	
9	Step on left foot, turning quarter turn left	◖
10	Stomp right foot beside left	❍
11	Step right foot back	
12	Touch left foot beside right	
13–16	Repeat steps 5–8	
17–24	Repeat steps 9–16	

(Contd.)

Beats	Movement	Direction
	Turn, Pause, Swivel Right and Left	
25	Step on left foot, turning quarter turn left	◖
26	Hold	
27	Step right foot beside left	
28	Hold	
	Weight on balls of both feet . . .	
29,30	Swivel heels right. Swivel heels centre	○
31,32	Swivel heels left. Swivel heels centre	
	Boot Hooks	
33,34	Tap right heel forward. Hook right foot over left shin	○
35,36	Tap right heel forward. Touch right foot beside left	
	Weave Right	
37,38	Step right foot to right side. Step left foot behind right	⇨
39,40	Step right foot to right side. Step left foot over *(in front of)* right	
41,42	Step right foot to right side. Step left foot behind right	
43,44	Step right foot to right side. Stomp left foot beside right *(weight on right foot)*	

Beats	Movement	Direction
	Weave Left	
45,46	Step left foot to left side. Step right foot behind left	⇦
47,48	Step left foot to left side. Step right foot over *(in front of)* left	
49,50	Step left foot to left side. Step right foot behind left	
51,52	Step left foot to left side. Stomp right foot beside left *(weight on right foot)*	

Begin again!

☆☆☆☆ Louisiana Hot Sauce ☆☆☆☆

Joanne Brady, Gordan Elliot,
Max Perry, Jo Thompson, USA

Two Wall

Beats	Movement	Direction
	Heel Struts and Heel Drops	
1&	Touch left heel forward, drop left toe lifting left heel and bending left knee	⇧
2&	Drop left heel to floor twice, shifting weight to left foot	
3&	Touch right heel forward, drop right toe lifting right heel and bending right knee	
4&	Drop right heel to floor twice, shifting weight to right foot	
	Cross, Unwind Half Right, Heel Twists, Clap	
5	Cross left foot over right	
6	Unwind half turn right, ending with feet apart	◗
7&8	Twist heels right, left, right	○
&	Clap	
	Cajun Jogs Forward and Clap	
9&10	Step forward left, right, left with weight on balls of feet	⇧
&	Hop on left foot, hitching right knee, clap	

Beats	Movement	Direction
11&12	Step forward right, left, right with weight on balls of feet	⇧
&	Hop on right foot, hitching left knee, clap	
	Back Skips and Forward Stomp	
13	Step left foot back, crossing slightly behind right	⇩
&	Hop on left foot hitching right knee	
14	Step right foot back, crossing slightly behind left	
&	Rock back onto left foot	❍
15	Stomp right foot right diagonal forward, bending right knee with weight over right foot *(Optional: arms out to sides, palms down)*	
16	Hold	
	Cross Rocks and Paddle Turn Left and Right	
17	Rock left foot across right, bending both knees	❍
&	Step weight back onto right foot *(straighten both legs)*	
18	Small step left to left side	
19	Rock right foot across left, bending both knees	

(Contd.)

Beats	Movement	Direction
&	Step weight back onto left foot *(straighten both legs)*	❍
20	Small step right to right side	
21	Rock left foot across right, bending both knees	
&	Step weight back onto right *(straighten both legs)*	
22	Small step left to left side, turning quarter turn left to begin a 360-degree turn left	●
&	Step right foot beside left on ball of foot	
23	Step on left foot continuing to turn	
&	Step right foot beside left on ball of foot	
24	Step on left foot, completing 360-degree turn *(now facing same wall as on step 17)*	
	Repeat last 8 counts with right foot leading . . .	
25	Rock right foot across left bending knees	❍
&	Step weight back onto left foot *(straighten both legs)*	
26	Small step right to right side	
27	Rock left foot across right, bending both knees	
&	Step weight back onto right foot	

Beats	Movement	Direction
	(straighten both legs)	
28	Small step left to left side	○
29	Rock right foot across left, bending both knees	
&	Step weight back onto left *(straighten both legs)*	
30	Small step right to right side, turning quarter turn right to begin a 360-degree turn right	●
&	Step left foot beside right on ball of foot	
31	Step on right foot continuing to turn	
&	Step left foot beside right on ball of foot	
32	Step on right, completing a 360-degree turn *(facing same wall as on steps 17&25)*	

Begin again!

☆☆☆☆ *Make Mine Country* ☆☆☆☆

Donna Wasnick, Tulare, USA — ***Two Wall***

If you're using Honky-Tonk Dancing Machine, *begin the dance after the 16-count intro.*

Beats	Movement	Direction
	Step Scoots	
1	Step right foot forward	⇧
2	Scoot forward on right, bringing left knee up and clap	
3	Step left foot forward	
4	Scoot forward on left, making a half turn and bringing right knee up, and clap	◖
5	Step right foot forward	⇧
6	Scoot forward on right, bringing left knee up and clap	
7	Step left foot forward	
8	Bring right knee up *(no scoot)* and clap	
9	Brush right foot forward	❍
10	Brush right foot back	
&	Step right foot back a little	
11	Cross left foot over right	
12	Point right toe to right side	

Beats	Movement	Direction
13	Cross right foot over left	◖
14	On balls of feet, make half turn to left *(weight on left)*	
15–16	Stomp right foot twice *(no weight change)*	

Shuffle Right, Pivot Turn

Beats	Movement	Direction
17	Step right foot forward	⇧
&	Step left next to right	
18	Step right foot forward	
19	Step left foot forward	
20	On balls of feet, make half turn to right *(weight on right)*	◗

Shuffle Left, Pivot Turn

Beats	Movement	Direction
21	Step left foot forward	⇧
&	Step right foot next to left	
22	Step left foot forward	
23	Step right foot forward	
24	On balls of feet, make half turn to left *(weight on left)*	◖

Diamond

Beats	Movement	Direction
25	Cross right foot over left	❍
26	Step left foot back	
27	Step right foot to right side	
28	Step left foot forward in front of right *(keep feet close together)*	

(Contd.)

Beats	Movement	Direction
	Twist and Turn	
29	Bend knees and swivel down, making half turn to right on balls of feet	❍
30	Swivel back up	
31	Bend knees and swivel down, making quarter turn to left on balls of feet	◢
32	Swivel back up	
	Heel Kicks	
33–34	Kick right heel forward twice	❍
35–36	Kick right heel back twice	
37	Kick right heel forward once	
38	On ball of left foot, make half turn to left and kick right foot back *(also known as a flick)*	◖
39	Stomp step right foot forward	
40	Stomp step left next to right	
	Heel Slaps	
41	Touch right heel forward	
42	Make quarter turn to left and slap right hand to right heel	◢
43	Step down on right foot, bending at knees, and bring fisted hands forward	❍
44	Come back up *(straighten legs)* and pull hands back	

Beats	Movement	Direction
45	Touch left heel forward	❍
46	Slap left hand to left heel	
47	Step down on left foot, bending at knees and bring fisted hands forward	
48	Come back up and pull hands back	

Begin again!

☆☆☆☆☆ Midnight Waltz ☆☆☆☆☆

Jo Thompson, Nashville, USA — ***Four Wall***

Beats	Movement	Direction
	Twinkle, Half Turn, Twinkle, Half Turn	
1	Cross left foot over right *(angle body right)*	❍
2	Step right foot beside left *(body centre)*	
3	Step left foot beside right *(body centre)*	
4	Cross right foot over left	
5	Pivot half turn right on right foot, stepping left foot beside right *(6 o'clock)*	⇦
6	Step right foot beside left	
7–12	Repeat steps 1–6 *(end facing 12 o'clock)*	
	3 Twinkles, Travel Left	
13–15	Repeat left foot 'Twinkle' steps 1–3	❍
16	Cross right foot over left *(angle body left)*	
17	Step left foot beside right *(body centre)*	
18	Step right foot beside left *(body centre)*	
19–21	Repeat left foot 'Twinkle' steps 1–3	
22	Cross right foot over left	
23	Step left foot to left side	
24	Step right foot behind left *(Optional full turn left on steps 23,24)*	

Beats	Movement	Direction
	Step, Slide Left and Right	
25	Step left foot to left side... long step	⇦
26,27	Slide right foot to meet left	
28	Step right foot to right side... long step	⇨
29,30	Slide left foot to meet right	
	Step, Hitch, Half Turn (x2)	
31	Step left foot forward	⇧
32,33	Kick right foot forward *(in a sweeping motion)*. Hold	
34	Step right foot back	
35	Turn half turn left *(on right foot)*, stepping left foot forward	◖
36	Step right foot beside left	
37–42	Repeat steps 31–36	
	Quarter Turn, Hesitation Step	
43	Step left foot, turning quarter turn left	◖
44,45	Step right foot beside left. Step left foot beside right	
46	Step right foot back	
47,48	Step left foot beside right. Step right foot beside left	⇩

Begin again!

☆☆☆☆☆ *Moonlight Waltz* ☆☆☆☆☆

Vera Brown, Campton, USA — ***One Wall***

Beats	Movement	Direction
	Forward Steps	
1	Step left foot forward	⇧
2	Step right foot forward	
3	Step left foot forward	
4	Step right foot forward	
5	Step left foot forward	
6	Step right foot forward	
	Back Steps	
7	Step left foot back	⇩
8	Step right foot back	
9	Step left foot back	
	Back Steps with Half Turn	
10	Step back on right foot, making half turn to right	◗
11	Step left foot forward	⇧
12	Step right foot forward	
13–15	Repeat steps 1–3	
16	Step back on right foot, making half turn to left	◖

Beats	Movement	Direction
17	Step left foot forward	⇧
18	Step right foot forward	
19–24	Repeat steps 1–6	
	Rolling Vine Left	
25	Step left foot to left, making half turn to left	⇦ ●
26	Step right foot to right of left, continuing turn	
27	Step left foot around right, completing full turn	
	Hip Sways	
28	Sway hips to right	○
29	Sway hips to left	
30	Sway hips to right	
31	Step left foot forward	⇧
32–33	Sweep right foot to right in circular motion with no weight change	
	Rolling Vine Right	
34	Step right foot to right, making half turn to right	● ⇨
35	Step left foot to left of right, continuing turn	

(Contd.)

Beats	Movement	Direction
36	Step right foot around left, completing full turn	
	Serpentines	
37	Step left foot diagonally in front of right	❍
38	Step right foot to right	
39	Turning slightly to left, step left foot to left	
40	Step right foot diagonally in front of left	❍
41	Step left foot in place	
42	Turning slightly to right, step right foot to right	
43–48	Repeat steps 37–42	
	Begin again!	

☆☆☆☆☆☆ *My Maria* ☆☆☆☆☆☆

Mike Camara and Dan Albro,
West Greenwich, USA

Four Wall

Beats	Movement	Direction
	Rock and Shuffle-step	
1	Rock forward on left foot	❍
2	Step right foot back	
3	Step left foot back	⇩
&	Step right next to left	
4	Step left foot back	
	Rock and Shuffle-step	
5	Rock back onto right foot	❍
6	Step left foot forward	
7	Step right foot forward	⇧
&	Step left next to right	
8	Step right foot forward	
	Half Turn and Shuffle-step	
9	Step left foot forward	◗
10	Make half turn to right, hooking right foot across left shin	
11	Step right foot forward	⇧
&	Step left next to right	
12	Step right foot forward	
13–16	Repeat steps 9–12	

(Contd.)

Beats	Movement	Direction
	Syncopated Chassé to Left	
17	Step left foot to left	⇦
18	Hold and clap	
&	Step right next to left	
19	Step left foot to left	
20	Touch right foot next to left and clap	
	Right Vine and Quarter Turn	
21	Step right foot to right	⇨
22	Step left foot behind right	
23	Step right foot to right	
&	Step left foot next to right	
24	Step right foot to right, making quarter turn to right	◗
	Half Turn	
25	Step left foot forward	
26	Make half turn to right	◗
	Turning Shuffle-step	
27	Step left foot forward	
&	Step right foot next to left, making quarter turn to right	◗
28	Step left foot back, making quarter turn to right	◗

Beats	Movement	Direction
	Rock and Shuffle-step	
29	Rock back on right foot	❍
30	Step left foot forward	
31	Step right foot forward	
&	Step left foot next to right	⇧
32	Step right foot forward	

Begin again!

☆☆☆☆ One Step Forward ☆☆☆☆

Four Wall

Beats	**Movement**	**Direction**
	Steps Forward and Backward	
1	Step left foot forward	⇧
2	Touch right foot beside left	
3	Step right foot back	⇩
4	Step left foot beside right	
5	Step right foot back	
6	Touch left foot beside right	
	Left Vine	
7	Step left foot to left side	⇦
8	Step right foot behind left	
9	Step left foot to left side	
10	Scuff right foot forward	
	Steps Forward and Backward	
11	Step right foot forward	⇧
12	Touch left foot beside right	
13	Step left foot back	⇩
14	Step right foot beside left	
15	Step left foot back	
16	Touch right foot beside left	

Beats	Movement	Direction
	Right Vine with Quarter Turn	
17	Step right foot to right side	⇨
18	Step left foot behind right	
19	Step right foot making quarter turn to right	◗
20	Scuff left foot forward	

Begin again!

☆☆☆☆☆☆ Ooh! Aah! ☆☆☆☆☆☆

Sal Gonzalez, Reedley, USA **Two Wall**

Id danced to Love Potion #9, *omit the first 16 counts on the 6th wall. Cue, listen for the trumpets in the music without the vocals.*

Beats	Movement	Direction
	Four Forward Shuffles	
1&2	Shuffle forward right, left , right	⇧
3&4	Shuffle forward left, right, left	
5–8	Repeat steps 1&2, 3&4	
	Turning Jazz Boxes	
9	Cross right foot over left	❍
10	Step left foot back	
11	Step right foot forward, turning quarter turn right	◗
12	Scuff left foot forward	
13	Cross left foot over right	❍
14	Step right foot back	
15	Step left foot forward, turning quarter turn left	◖
16	Touch right foot beside left	

Travelling Side Shuffles with Half Turns, Kick-Ball-Change

Beats	Movement	Direction
17&18	Shuffle to right side, right, left, right	⇨
&	Turn half turn right	
19&20	Shuffle to left side, left, right, left	
&	Turn half turn left	
21&22	Shuffle to right side, right, left, right	
23	Kick left foot forward	
&	Step on ball of left foot	❍
24	Step right foot in place	
	Repeat steps 17–24 with left foot leading . . .	
25&26	Shuffle to left side, left, right, left	⇦
&	Turn half turn left	
27&28	Shuffle to right side, right, left, right	
&	Turn half turn right	
29&30	Shuffle to left side, left, right, left	
31	Kick right foot forward	
&	Step on ball of right foot	❍
32	Step left foot in place	
	Rock Forward and Back, Two Quarter Turns Left	
33	Rock forward onto right foot	❍
34	Step left foot in place	
35	Rock back onto right foot	
36	Step left foot in place	

(Contd.)

Beats	Movement	Direction
37	Step right foot forward, turning quarter turn left	◖
38	Step left foot in place	
39,40	Repeat 37,38	
	(Optional hip rolls on steps 37–40)	

Forward, Walk, Stomp, Body Roll

Beats	Movement	Direction
41–44	Walk forward, right, left, right, left	⇧
45	Stomp right foot beside left	
46–48	Roll body counter-clockwise, ending with weight on left foot	❍

**6th Wall begins at step 17*

Repeat shorter pattern (steps 17–48) until music ends

☆☆☆☆☆ Psycho Cowboy ☆☆☆☆☆

Kathy J. Dubois, USA — ***Four Wall***

Beats	Movement	Direction
	Turning Shuffle, Toe Touch, Clap	
1	Step right foot to right side	⇨
&	Step left foot beside right	
2	Step right foot to right side, turning half turn right	◗
3	Step left foot to left side	⇦
4	Touch right toe front	
5,6	Touch right toe to right side. Clap	○
7–12	Repeat steps 1–6	
	Shuffles and Scoots	
13&14	Shuffle forward, right, left, right	⇧
15&16	Shuffle forward, left, right, left	
&	Scoot back on left foot	⇩
17	Step right foot back	
&	Scoot back on right foot	
18	Step back on left foot	
&	Scoot back on left foot	
19	Touch right toe back	
&20	Repeat steps &19	
	Hip Sways, Cross Turn and Shoot!	
21	Step right foot to right, swaying hips	○

(Contd.)

Beats	Movement	Direction
	right. Slap both hands down across thighs	○
&	Slap both hands up across thighs	
22	Step left foot beside right, swaying hips left. Clap	
23	Step right foot to right, turning quarter turn left, sway hips right Slap both hands down across thighs	
&	Slap both hands up across thighs	
24	Step left foot beside right swaying hips left. Clap	
25	Cross right foot over left	
26	Unwind half turn left *(on balls of*	◖
27	*both feet)*	
	Cross arms, right hand to left hip,	
28	left hand to right hip	
	Jump forward, feet apart, shoot with both hands	⇧

Begin again!

☆☆☆☆ Rattlesnake Shake ☆☆☆☆

Hillbilly Rick and Linda Moseby, Haubstadt, USA **_Four Wall_**

If using Rattlesnake Shake, *begin the dance when you hear the vocals 'Get up every morning'.*

Beats	Movement	Direction
	Triple-step through the Baby Rattlers	
1&2	Triple-step in place right, left, right, prancing on balls of feet, angle body slightly right	○
3&4	Triple-step in place left, right, left, prancing on balls of feet, angle body slightly left	
	Chassé, Touch, Step, Slide Forward, Step, Touch	
5,6	Step right foot to right side. Step left foot beside right	⇨
7,8	Step right foot to right side. Touch left foot beside right	
9	Step left foot left diagonal forward *(11 o'clock)*	⬁
10	Slide right foot up beside left	
11	Step left foot left diagonal forward *(11 o'clock)*	
12	Touch right foot beside left	

(Contd.)

Beats	Movement	Direction
	Chassé, Touch, Step, Slide Backward, Step, Touch	
13–16	Repeat steps 5–8	
17	Step left foot left diagonal backwards *(7 o'clock)*	
18	Slide right foot beside left	
19	Step left foot left diagonal backwards *(7 o'clock)*	
20	Touch right foot beside left	
	Jazz Jumps Back, Clap, Ronde Half Turn Right	
&21,22	Right foot small step back. Left foot small step back, clap	
&23,24	Repeat steps &21,22 *Weight on left foot . . .*	
25	Slide right toe forward	
26,27	Sweep right toe *(as if drawing a circle)* around clockwise, turning half turn right on left foot	
28	Touch right foot beside left	
	Rattlesnake Shake	
	(down twice, up twice, down twice, up twice) *For styling: while bumping hips, pump hands like shaking a rattle, shake shoulders*	

Beats	Movement	Direction
29&30	Slide right foot to right forward diagonal, bend knees, angle body left bump hips to right twice	❍
31&32	Slide right foot back to left Straighten knees and shake shoulders twice	
33–36	Repeat steps 29–32	
	Two Quarter Turns	
37	Step right foot forward	
38	Pivot quarter turn left, swinging hips right	◖
39,40	Repeat steps 37,38	◖
	Right Vine, Scuff, Left Vine with Turn, Scuff	
41,42	Step right foot to right side, step left foot behind right	⇨
43,44	Step right foot to right side, scuff left foot forward	
45,46	Step left foot to left side, step right foot behind left	⇦
47,48	Step left foot to left side, turning quarter turn left, scuff right foot forward *(Optional: 1 quarter turn for steps 45–48, stepping left, right, left, scuff right forward.)*	◖

Begin again!

☆☆☆☆☆☆☆☆☆ Ridin' ☆☆☆☆☆☆☆☆☆

Dave Ingram, Ottawa, Canada — ***Four Wall***

Beats	Movement	Direction
	Side Shuffle and Rock	
1	Step right foot to right side	⇨
&	Step left foot beside right	
2	Step right foot to right side	
3	Rock back onto left foot	❍
4	Rock forward onto right foot	
5	Step left foot to left side	⇦
&	Step right foot beside left	
6	Step left foot to left side	
7	Rock back onto right foot	❍
8	Rock forward onto left foot	
	Shuffle Forward Half Turn, Shuffle Forward Quarter Turn	
9	Step right foot forward	⇧
&	Step left foot beside right	
10	Step right foot forward	
11	Step left foot forward	
12	Pivot half turn right	◗
13	Step left foot forward	⇧
&	Step right foot beside left	

Beats	Movement	Direction
14	Step left foot forward	⇧
15	Step right foot forward	
16	Pivot quarter turn left	◢

17–24	Repeat steps 9–16	

Flick Kick Quarter Turn and Stomp

25	Kick right foot forward	○
26	Kick right foot behind, turning quarter turn left	◢
27,28	Stomp right foot, stomp left foot	○

Ronde Half Turn Left

29	Step right foot back	
30,31	Sweep left toe around, turning half turn left	◖
32	Step left foot beside right	

Begin again!

☆☆☆ Rock Around the Clock ☆☆☆

Four Wall

Beats	Movement	Direction
	Toe Touches and Cross Steps	
1	Touch right toe to right side	❍
2	Touch right toe in place	
3	Touch right toe to right side	
4	Hold	
5	Cross right foot behind left	⇦
6	Step left foot to left side	
7	Cross right foot in front of left	
8	Hold	
	Repeat steps 1–8 with left foot leading . . .	
9	Touch left toe to left side	❍
10	Touch left toe in place	
11	Touch left toe to left side	
12	Hold	
13	Cross left foot behind right	⇨
14	Step right foot to right side	
15	Cross left foot in front of right	
16	Hold	

Beats	Movement	Direction
	Rock Steps, Lock Steps	
17	Rock forward onto right foot	❍
18	Rock back onto left foot	
19	Step right foot in place	
20	Hold	
21	Step left foot behind right foot	⇩
22	Lock right foot over left	
23	Step left foot back	
24	Hold	
25	Rock back onto right foot	❍
26	Rock forward onto left foot	
27	Step right foot in place	
28	Hold	
29	Step left foot in front of right	⇧
30	Lock right foot behind left	
31	Step left foot forward	
32	Hold	
	Sugarfoots Right and Left	
33	Point right toe to left instep	❍
34	Touch right heel to left instep	
35	Step right foot in place	
36	Hold	

(Contd.)

Beats	Movement	Direction
37	Point left toe to right instep	◑
38	Touch left heel to right instep	
39	Step left foot in place	
40	Hold	
	Coaster Step	
41	Step right foot back	◑
42	Step left foot beside right	
43	Step right foot forward	
44	Hold	
	Three-quarter Turn Left	
45–47	Triple-step in place left, right, left, turning three-quarter turn left	◕
48	Hold	

Begin again!

☆☆☆☆☆☆☆ Rock It ☆☆☆☆☆☆☆

Hillbilly Rick, Haubstadt, USA ***Two Wall***

Beats	Movement	Direction
1	Swivel heels to right and bump hip to right	❍
2	Bump hip to right again	
3	Swivel heels to left and bump hip to left	
4	Bump hip to left again	
5–6	As you twist body downward, swivel heels to right, then to left	
7–8	As you twist body upward, swivel heels to right, then left	

Beats	Movement	Direction
9	Step back on right and turn body to right at 45-degree angle	⇩
10	Clap	
11	Step back on left and turn body to left at 45-degree angle	
12	Clap	
13	Step back on right and turn body to right at 45-degree angle	
14	Clap	
15	Step back on left and turn body to left at 45-degree angle	
16	Clap	

(Contd.)

Beats	Movement	Direction
17&18	Right shuffle-step forward *(right, left, right)*	⇧
19&20	Left shuffle-step forward *(left, right, left)*	
21	Step forward on right	
22	Make half turn to left, ending with weight on left foot	◖
23&24	Right shuffle-step forward *(right, left, right)*	⇧
25&26	Left shuffle-step forward *(left, right, left)*	
27	Step forward on right	
28	Make half turn to left, ending with weight on left foot	◖

Jazz Square

29	Cross right over left	❍
30	Step back on left	
31	Step to right with right foot	
32	Step left foot beside right	
33–36	Repeat steps 29–32	

Vine Right

37	Step to right with right	⇨
38	Step behind right with left	
39	Step to right with right	
40	Scuff left foot	

Beats	Movement	Direction
	Vine Left with Half Turn	
41	Step to left with left	⇦
42	Step behind left with right	
43	Step to left with left and make half turn to left	◖
44	Scuff right foot	
	Vine Right	
45	Step to right with right	⇨
46	Step behind right with left	
47	Step to right with right	
48	Stomp left foot	

Begin again!

☆☆☆☆☆☆ Rockin' Rebel ☆☆☆☆☆☆

Linda DeFord, Knoxville, USA — ***Four Wall***

Remember that the '&' symbol means that you take 3 steps in only 2 beats. Pay attention to turns – it's easy to get twisted around – and remember where the original wall was at the start.

Beats	Movement	Direction
	Chassé Right	
1	Step right foot to right side	⇨
&	Quickly step left foot next to right	
2	Step right foot to right side	
3	Rock back on left foot behind right	❍
4	Rock forward on right foot, facing straight again	
	Chassé Left	
5	Step left foot to left side	⇦
&	Quickly step right foot next to left	
6	Step left foot to left side	
7	Rock back on right foot behind left	❍
8	Rock forward on left, facing straight	
	Shuffle and Half Turn	
9&10	Right shuffle-step forward *(right, left, right)*	⇧
11	Step left foot forward	

Beats	Movement	Direction
12	Make half turn to right, shifting weight to right foot	◗
	Shuffle and Quarter Turn	
13&14	Left shuffle-step forward *(left, right, left)*	⇧
15	Step right foot forward	
16	Make quarter turn to left, shifting weight to left foot	◖
	Shuffle and Half Turn	
17&18	Right shuffle-step forward *(right, left, right)*	⇧
19	Step left foot forward	
20	Make half turn to right, shifting weight to right foot	◗
	Shuffle and Quarter Turn	
21&22	Left shuffle-step forward *(left, right, left)*	⇧
23	Step right foot forward	
24	Make quarter turn to left, stomping left foot *(shift weight to left foot on this move)*	◖
	Kick Turn	
25	Kick right foot forward, twisting into...	
&	...a quarter turn to left on ball of left foot	◖

(Contd.)

Beats	Movement	Direction
26	Step right foot next to left	❍
27	Step left foot to left	❍
&	Kick right foot forward	
28	Quickly step right foot behind left; shift weight to right foot as you do so	
29	Kick left foot forward	❍
&	Swing left foot behind right	
30	Switch weight to left foot *(still behind right)*	
	Unwind Legs	
31–32	Make half turn to left by pressing into floor with ball of right foot and ending with weight on left foot	◖
	Begin again!	

☆☆☆☆☆☆☆☆ Rodeo ☆☆☆☆☆☆☆☆☆

Dale White ***Two Wall***

Beats	Movement	Direction
	Kick, Kick, Cross-Ball-Change	
1,2	Kick right foot forward twice	❍
3	Step right foot behind left	
&	Step left foot to left side	
4	Step right foot beside left	
	Repeat steps 1–4 with left foot leading . . .	
5,6	Kick left foot forward twice	❍
7	Step left foot behind right	
&	Step right foot to right side	
8	Step left foot beside right	
	Quarter Turn, Shuffle Forward	
&	Pivot quarter turn right on ball of left foot	◗
9&10	Shuffle forward, right, left, right	⇧
11&12	Shuffle forward, left, right, left	
13–16	Repeat steps 9–12	
	Quarter Turn, Chassé Left	
17	Cross right foot over left, turning quarter turn left	◖

(Contd.)

Beats	Movement	Direction
&	Step left foot to left side	⇦
18	Cross right foot over left	
&	Step left foot to left side	
19	Cross right foot over left	
&	Step left foot to left side	
20	Cross right foot over left	
&	Step left foot to left side	
	Kick, Kick, Cross-Ball-Change	
21,22	Kick left foot forward twice	❍
23	Step left foot behind right	
&	Step right foot to right side	
24	Step left foot beside right	
	Right Heel Hook, Heel, Together	
25,26	Touch right heel forward. Hook right foot over left shin	❍
27,28	Touch right heel forward. Step right foot beside left	
	Left Heel Hook, Heel Together	
29,30	Touch left heel forward. Hook left foot over right shin	❍
31,32	Touch left heel forward. Step left foot beside right	
	Jazz Box with Turn	
33	Step right foot forward.	

Beats	Movement	Direction
34	Cross left foot over right	
35,36	Step right foot back. Step left foot turning quarter turn left	
37–40	Repeat steps 33–36	
41–44	Repeat steps 25–28	
	Right Heel, Toe, Heel, Touch Across	
45,46	Touch right heel forward. Touch right toe back	
47,48	Touch right heel forward. Hook right foot across left, set toe on floor	

Begin again!

☆☆☆☆☆☆☆☆☆ Romeo ☆☆☆☆☆☆☆☆☆

Four Wall

Beats	Movement	Direction
	Right Vine	
1	Step right foot to right side	⇨
2	Cross left foot in front of right	
3	Step right foot to right side	
4	Touch left foot beside right	
	Reverse Left Vine	
5	Step left foot to left side	⇦
6	Cross right foot in front of left	
7	Step left foot to left side	
8	Touch right foot beside left	
	Rolling Right Vine (360-degree Turn)	
9	Step right foot to right side, turning quarter turn right *(3 o'clock)*	● ⇨
10	Swing left foot forward, continuing to turn another quarter turn right *(6 o'clock)* transfer weight to left foot	
11	Pivot on left foot, swing right back, completing turn to face *(12 o'clock)*	
12	Touch left foot beside right	

Beats	Movement	Direction
	Rolling Left Vine (360-degree Turn)	
13	Step left foot to left side, turning quarter turn left *(9 o'clock)*	⇦ ●
14	Swing right foot forward, continuing to turn another quarter turn left *(6 o'clock)* transfer weight to right foot	
15	Pivot on right foot, swing left back, completing turn to face *(12 o'clock)*	
16	Touch right foot beside left	
	Walk Backwards	
17–19	Walk back, right, left, right	⇩
20	Touch left foot beside right	
	Drag Steps Forward	
21	Step left foot forward	⇧
22	Slide right foot up to meet left	
23,24	Repeat steps 21,22	
	'Hands On Jeans'	
25	Place right hand on right back pocket	❍
26	Place left hand on left back pocket	
27	Place right hand on right front pocket *(down low)*	
28	Place left hand on left front pocket *(down low)*	
29–32	Body roll twice *(with attitude!)*	

(Contd.)

Beats	Movement	Direction
	Double Heel, Toe	
33,34	Tap right heel forward twice	❍
35,36	Tap right toe behind twice	
	Star with Right Foot	
37,38	Touch right toe forward. Touch right toe to right side	❍
39	Lock right foot behind left, right toe touching the floor	
40	Swivel quarter turn left with right foot in locked position	◖

Begin again!

☆☆☆☆☆ Rompin' Stompin' ☆☆☆☆☆

Robert Royston, Dublin, USA — ***Two Wall***

Beats	Movement	Direction
	Heel Rock Forward, Rock Back	
1	Rock forward onto right heel	○
2	Step left foot in place	
3	Rock back onto right foot	
4	Step left foot in place	
	Shimmy, Jump, Jump	
5,6	Step right foot to right side. Hold Shimmy on 5,6	⇨
7,8	Feet still apart, jump to right side twice	
	Quarter Turns	
9,10	Step right foot forward. Hold	
11,12	Quarter turn left. Hold	◖
13–16	Repeat steps 9–12	
17–32	Repeat steps 1–16	
	Kick, Cross Rock, Rock, Rock (Right and Left)	
33	Kick right foot forward left across left foot	
34	Cross right foot over left, rocking weight onto right foot	

(Contd.)

Beats	Movement	Direction
35	Rock back onto left foot	❍
36	Rock forward onto right foot	
37	Kick left foot forward across right foot	
38	Cross left foot over right, rocking weight onto left foot	❍
39	Rock back onto right foot	
40	Rock forward onto left foot	
41–48	Repeat steps 33–40 *(The kicks are fast, angle body slightly to the left and right 45 degrees, however, you still face original wall.)*	

Windmill Turn

Beats	Movement	Direction
49	Turn quarter turn left on ball of left foot, swinging right foot forward	◖
50	Hold	
51	Clap	
52	Hold	
53	Turn quarter turn left on ball of right foot, swinging left foot back	◖
54	Hold	
55	Clap	
56	Hold	

Right Weave

Beats	Movement	Direction
57,58	Step right foot to right side. Hold	⇨
59,60	Cross left foot over right. Hold	

Beats	Movement	Direction
61,62	Step right foot to right side. Cross left foot behind right	
63	Step right foot forward, turning quarter turn right	◖
64	Stomp left foot beside right *(weight on left)*	❍

Begin again!

☆☆☆☆☆☆ Six Shooter ☆☆☆☆☆☆

Two Wall

Beats	Movement	Direction
	Heel Twists	
1	Twist heels left	❍
2	Twist heels centre	
3,4	Stomp right foot twice *(no weight on stomp)*	
	Heel Hooks	
5	Tap right heel forward	❍
6	Hook right foot over left shin	
7	Tap right heel forward	
8	Step right beside left *(weight on right foot)*	
9	Tap left heel forward	❍
10	Hook left foot over right shin	
11	Tap left heel forward	
12	Touch left toe behind	
	Rolling Left Vine and Side Touches	
13	Step left foot forward, turning quarter turn left	⇦ ◢
14	Step right foot forward, turning half turn left	◖
15	Step left foot forward, turning quarter turn left	◢

Beats	Movement	Direction
16	Step right foot beside left	❍
17	Touch left foot out to left side	❍
18	Step left foot beside right	
19	Touch right foot out to right side	
20	Touch right foot beside left	
	Rolling Right Vine and Side Touches	
21	Step right foot forward, turning quarter turn right	⇨ ◗
22	Step left forward, turning half turn right	◗
23	Step right foot forward, turning quarter turn right	◗
24	Touch left beside right	❍
	Step, Lock, Step, Half Turn	
25	Step left foot forward	⇧
26	Drag right foot up and lock behind left	
27	Step left foot forward	
28	Swivel half turn to left	◖
	Step, Drag, Step, Drag	
29	Step right foot forward	⇧
30	Drag left foot up beside right	
31	Step right foot forward	
32	Drag left foot up beside right	

Begin again!

☆☆☆☆☆ Slappin' Leather ☆☆☆☆☆

Gayle Brandon, San Juan Capistrano, USA **_Four Wall_**

Choreographed in 1978, you will see this dance everywhere. Different clubs may have variations, but this is the original.

Beats	Movement	Direction
	Pigeon Toes	
1	With weight on balls of feet, turn heels out	❍
2	Bring heels back together	
3	Turn heels out	
4	Bring heels back together	
	Side-steps	
5	Point right toe to right side	❍
6	Bring right foot back next to left	
7	Point left toe to left side	
8	Bring left foot back next to right	
9	Point right toe to right side	
10	Bring right foot back next to left	
11	Point left toe to left side	
12	Bring left foot back next to right	
	Taps	
13,14	Tap right heel directly in front twice	❍
15,16	Tap right toe directly behind twice	

Beats	Movement	Direction
	Slappin' Leather	
17	Point right toe in front	○
18	Point right toe to right side	
19	Cross right leg up behind left knee and slap boot with left hand	
20	Point right toe to right side	
21	Cross right leg up behind left knee and slap boot with left hand, again	
22	Point right toe to right side	
23	Cross right leg in front of left knee, slap boot with left hand as you do a quarter turn left *(pivot on ball of left foot)*	◖
24	With right leg still in air, turn knee so boot goes a little to right and slap boot with right hand	
	Right Vine	
25	Step to the right on right foot	⇨
26	Step behind right on left foot	
27	Step to the right on right foot	
28	Hop or scuff left heel next to right *(Variation: cross left leg behind right knee and slap boot with right hand.)*	
	Left Vine	
29	Step to the left on left foot	⇦
30	Step behind left on right foot	

(Contd.)

Beats	Movement	Direction
31	Step to the left on left foot	⇦
32	Hop or scuff right heel next to left *(Variation: cross right leg behind left knee and slap boot with left hand.)*	
33	Step back on right	⇩
34	Left	
35	Right	
36	Hop on right	
37	Step forward on left	⇧
38	Step forward on right	
39	Step forward on left	
40	Stomp right foot beside left foot	

Begin again!

☆☆☆☆☆ Smokey Places ☆☆☆☆☆

Michele Perron, USA ***Four Wall***

Beats	Movement	Direction
	Rumba Box	
1	Step left foot to left side	⇦
2	Step right foot beside left	
3	Step left foot forward	⇧
4	Hold	
5	Step right foot to right side	⇨
6	Step left foot beside right	
7	Step right foot back	⇩
8	Hold	
	Side, Together, Side Hold	
9	Step left foot to left side	⇦
10	Step right foot beside left	
11	Step left foot to left side.	
12	Hold	
	Behind and Cross, Touch	
13	Cross right foot behind left	⇦
14	Step left foot to left side	
15	Cross right foot over left	
16	Touch left toe to left side	

(Contd.)

Beats	Movement	Direction
	Cross, Touch, Step and Tap	
17	Cross left foot behind right	❍
18	Touch right toe out to right side	
19	Cross right foot over left	
20	Tap left toe behind right foot	
	Backward Half Turn and Tap	
21	Step left foot back	
22	Step onto right, turning half turn right	◗
23	Step left foot forward	
24	Tap right toe behind left foot	
	Backward Half Turn and Tap	
25	Step right foot back	
26	Step onto left, turning half turn left	◖
27	Step right foot forward	
28	Tap left toe behind right foot	
	Quarter Turn Right and Hip Sways	
29	Step left foot back	
30	Step onto right, turning quarter turn right	◔
31	Step left foot beside right, sway hips left	
32	Sway hips right, changing weight to right foot	

Begin again!

☆☆☆☆☆ The Snakebite ☆☆☆☆☆

Four Wall

Beats	Movement	Direction
1	Split heels *(with weight on balls of feet, separate heels)*	◯
2	Bring heels together	
3	Tap right heel forward	
4	Bring right foot back next to left	
5	Split heels	
6	Bring heels together	
7	Tap left heel forward	
8	Bring left foot back next to right	

Beats	Movement	Direction
	Kicks	
9	Step forward on left foot, make half turn to right	◗
10	Kick right foot forward	
11	Step back on right foot	
12	Kick left foot	
13	Step forward on left foot, make half turn to right	◗
14	Kick right foot forward	
15	Step back on right foot	
16	Touch left foot beside right	

(Contd.)

Beats	Movement	Direction
	Left Vine	
17	Step to the left with left foot	⇦
18	Cross right foot behind left foot	
19	Step to the left with left foot	
20	Stomp right foot beside left	

Beats	Movement	Direction
	Swivels and Hook	
21	Swivel heels right *(weight on balls of feet)*	❍
22	Swivel toes right *(keep weight on heels)*	
23	Tap left heel forward	
24	Cross left foot in front of right shin	
25	Tap left heel forward	
26	Bring left foot back next to right *(but don't change weight)*	

Beats	Movement	Direction
	Rock Steps and Turn	
27	Left step forward	❍
28	Rock back on right foot	
29	Rock forward on left foot	
30	Stomp right foot next to left	
31	Step back on right foot	⇩
32	Slide left foot back next to right	
33	Step back on right foot, making a quarter turn to right	◗
34	Place left foot beside right	

Begin again!

☆☆☆ Swamp Thang ☆☆☆

(a.k.a. Heart like a Wheel)

Max Perry, Danbury, USA **Four Wall**

Advanced dancers may want to replace the in-place shuffles at steps 7&8 and 11&12 – the first to the right and the second to the left.

Beats	Movement	Direction
	Rock Step, Coaster Step	
1	Rock forward on left foot	❍
2	Step right foot in place	
3	Step left foot back	❍
&	Step right foot next to left	
4	Step left foot forward	
	Rock Step, Coaster Step	
5	Rock forward on right foot	❍
6	Step left foot in place	
7	Step right foot back	
&	Step left foot next to right	❍
8	Step right foot forward	
	Rock Side, Shuffle Step	
9	Rock step to left side with left foot	⇦
10	Step right foot in place	
11	Step left foot next to right	❍
&	Step right foot in place	
12	Step left foot in place	

(Contd.)

Beats	Movement	Direction
	Rock Side, Shuffle Step	
13	Rock step to right side with right foot	⇨
14	Step left foot in place	○
15	Step right foot next to left	
&	Step left foot in place	
16	Step right foot in place	
	Vine Left	
17	Step left foot to left side	⇦
18	Cross right foot behind left	
19	Step left foot to left side	
20	Step right foot next to left	
	Left Shuffle	
21	Step left foot to left side	⇦
&	Step right foot next to right quickly	
22	Step left foot to left side	
23	Rock back on right foot	○
24	Step left foot in place	
	Right Vine	
25	Step right foot to right side	⇨
26	Cross left foot behind right	
27	Step right foot to right side	
28	Step left foot next to right	

Beats	Movement	Direction
	Right Shuffle	
29	Step right foot to right side	⇨
&	Step left foot next to right quickly	
30	Step right foot to right side	
31	Rock back on left foot	○
32	Step right foot in place	
	Syncopated Chassé	
33	Step left foot to left side	⇦
34	Hold and clap	
&	Step right foot next to left	
35	Step left foot to left side	
36	Hold and clap	
&	Step right foot next to left	
37	Step left foot forward, making quarter turn to left	◤
38	Step right foot forward and make half turn to left	◖
39	Step left foot next to right	
40	Stomp right foot *(shifting weight to right foot)*	○

Begin again!

☆☆☆☆ Tennessee Twister ☆☆☆☆

Two Wall

Beats	Movement	Direction
	Heel Twists	
1,2	Twist heels right, hold	❍
3,4	Twist heels left, hold	
5	Twist heels right	
6	Twist heels left	
7	Twist heels right	
8	Twist heels centre	
	Heel and Toe Taps	
9,10	Tap right heel forward, twice	❍
11,12	Tap right toe behind, twice	
	Drag Steps with Half Turn	
13	Step right foot forward	⇧
14	Drag left up behind right	
15,16	Repeat steps 13,14	
17	Step right foot forward	
18	Half turn to right on ball of right foot	◗
19	Step left foot forward	⇧
20	Drag right up behind left	
21,22	Repeat steps 19,20	
23	Step left foot forward	
24	Half turn to left on ball of left foot	◖

Beats	Movement	Direction
	Right Vine with Half Turn	
25	Step right foot to right side	⇨
26	Step left foot behind right	
27	Step right foot to right side	
28	Half turn to left on ball of right foot	◖
29	Step left foot to left side	⇦
30	Step right foot behind left	
31	Step left foot to left side	
32	Stomp right foot beside left	

Begin again!

☆☆☆☆☆ Texas Twister ☆☆☆☆☆

Four Wall

Beats	Movement	Direction
	Shuffle Left and Rock	
1	Step left foot to left side	⇦
&	Step right foot beside left	
2	Step left foot to left side	
3	Rock back onto right foot	❍
4	Rock forward onto left foot	
	Shuffle Right and Rock	
5	Step right foot to right side	⇨
&	Step left foot beside right	
6	Step right foot to right side	
7	Rock back onto left foot	❍
8	Rock forward onto right foot	
	Left Shuffle Forward and Pivot Turn	
9	Step left foot forward	⇧
&	Step right foot beside left	
10	Step left foot forward	
11	Step right foot forward	
12	Pivot half turn left, ending with weight on left foot	◖

Beats	Movement	Direction
	Right Shuffle Forward and Pivot Turn	
13	Step right foot forward	
&	Step left foot beside right	
14	Step right foot forward	
15	Step left foot forward	
16	Pivot half turn right, ending with weight on right foot	
	Left Vine	
17	Step left foot to left side	
18	Step right foot behind left	
19	Step left foot to left side	
20	Touch right foot beside left	
	Right Vine with Quarter Turn	
21	Step right foot to right side	
22	Step left foot behind right	
23	Step right foot to right side, turning quarter turn right	
24	Touch left foot beside right	
	Syncopated Jumps	
&	Short jump forward on left foot	
25,26	Step right foot beside left. Clap	
&	Short jump back on right foot	
27,28	Step left foot beside right. Clap	

(Contd.)

Beats	Movement	Direction
	Heel Twists	
29	Twist heels left	O
30	Twist heels right	
31	Twist heels left	
32	Twist heels centre	

Begin again!

☆☆☆☆☆ Thin Sole Shoes ☆☆☆☆☆

Susie Hollingsworth — ***Four Wall***

Beats	Movement	Direction
	Four Strut Steps	
1,2	Step forward on right toes. Lower right heel down	⇧
3,4	Step forward on left toes. Lower left heel down	
5–8	Repeat steps 1–4	
	Polka Twice	
9&10	Shuffle toward diagonal right *(2 o'clock)*, right, left, right	⬀
11&12	Shuffle toward diagonal left *(10 o'clock)*, left, right, left	⬁
	Kick-Ball-Change, Step, Quarter Turn	
13&14	Right kick-ball-change	❍
15	Step right foot forward	
16	Pivot quarter turn left	◖
	Pivot, Cross Four Times, Pivot	
17,18	Step right foot forward. Pivot half turn left	◖
19,20	Cross right foot over left. Cross left foot over right	

(Contd.)

Beats	Movement	Direction
21,22	Repeat steps 19,20	❍
23,24	Repeat steps 17,18	
	Jazz Box	
25,26	Cross right foot over left. Step left foot back	❍
27,28	Step right foot to right side. Step left foot beside right	
	Kick-Ball-Change (x2)	
29–32	Right kick-ball-change twice	❍
	Cross, Strut	
33	Cross right foot over left on ball of right foot	⇦
34	Step down on right heel	
35	Step on ball of left foot beside right	
36	Step down on left heel	
37–40	Repeat steps 33–36	
	Jazz Box with Quarter Turn	
41	Cross right foot over left, turning quarter turn left	◗
42	Step left foot back	
43	Step right foot to right side	❍
44	Step left foot beside right	

Beats	Movement	Direction
	Strut in Place	
45	Step onto ball of right foot beside left	○
46	Step right heel down	
47	Step onto ball of left foot beside right	
48	Step left heel down	
	Chassé Right, Touch	
49,50	Step right foot to right side. Step left foot beside right	⇨
51,52	Step right foot to right side. Touch left foot beside right	
	Chassé Left, Touch	
53,54	Step left foot to left side. Step right foot beside left	⇦
55,56	Step left foot to left side. Touch right foot beside left	

Begin again!

☆☆☆☆☆ The T. L. Shake ☆☆☆☆☆

Donna Wasnick, Tulare, USA **Two Wall**

This dance is designed for If The Good Die Young. *Begin after a 32-count intro. in song. Dance the first part as choreographed three times. There will then be a 16-count music break. During those 16 beats, dance the Shimmy Shakes (see at the end of the instructions), then dance the original 32 steps until the end of the song.*

Beats	Movement	Direction
	Heel Steps	
1	Touch right heel forward	
2	Step down on ball of right foot	
3	Make half turn left on ball of right foot and touch left heel forward	◖
4	Step down on ball of left foot	
5	Touch right heel forward	
6	Step down on ball of right foot	
7	Make half turn left on ball of right foot and touch left heel forward	◖
8	Step down on ball of left foot	

Beats	Movement	Direction
	Shuffle Turns	
9&10	Right shuffle-step forward *(right, left, right)*	⇧
11	Step forward on left foot	
12	Make half turn to right	◗

Beats	Movement	Direction
	(switching weight to right foot)	
13&14	Left shuffle-step forward *(left, right, left)*	⇧
15	Step forward on right foot	
16	Make quarter turn to left on balls of both feet *(shift weight to left foot)*	◖
	Hip Shakes	
17	Step right foot to right and shake right hip	❍
18	Shake right hip again	
19	Make quarter turn to right on ball of right foot and touch left next to right	◗
20	Hold	
21	Step left foot to left and shake left hip	❍
22	Shake left hip again	
23	Touch right foot next to left	
24	Hold	
	Back Hip Shakes	
25	Step back on right foot and shake right hip	⇩
26	Shake right hip again	
27	Step back on left foot and shake left hip	
28	Shake left hip again	
	Hip Rolls	
29	Roll hips forward	❍

(Contd.)

Beats	Movement	Direction
30	Roll hips back	❍
31	Roll hips forward	
32	Roll hips back *(end with weight on left foot)*	
	Shimmy Shakes	
1,2	Step right foot to right side and shake right hip twice	⇨
3,4	Step left next to right and hold	
5,6	Step right foot to right side and shake right hip twice	
7,8	Step left next to right and hold	
9,10	Step left foot to left side and shake left hip twice	⇦
11,12	Step right next to left and hold	
13,14	Step left foot to left side and shake left hip twice	
15,16	Step right next to left and hold	

Begin again!

☆☆☆☆☆ Tobacco Boogie ☆☆☆☆☆

Martie and Jim Ferrazzano, USA **_Four Wall_**

Beats	Movement	Direction
	Step, Hold, Twists, Pivot Turn	
1,2	Step right foot forward. Hold	⇧
3,4	Step left foot directly in front of right. Hold	
5	On balls of both feet, twist heels in	
&	Twist heels out	
6	Twist heels in	
7	Step right foot forward	
8	Pivot half turn left	◖
	Hop, Clap, Unwind, Hop, Clap	
9	Hop back slightly, landing both feet together	⇩
10	Clap	
11	Cross right foot over left	
12	Unwind half turn left	◖
13	Hop back slightly, landing both feet together	⇩
14	Clap	
15,16	Repeat steps 13,14	
	Diagonal Heel Touches	
&	Step left foot back diagonally *(7 o'clock)*	❍

(Contd.)

Beats	Movement	Direction
17	Touch right heel diagonally forward *(1 o'clock)*	❍
&	Step right foot in place	
18	Step left foot beside right	
&	Step right foot diagonally back *(5 o'clock)*	
19	Touch left heel diagonally forward *(11 o'clock)*	
&	Step left foot in place	
20	Step right foot beside left	
&21–24	Repeat steps &17–20	

Hop Back, Out-Out, In-In, Jazz Box with Turn

Beats	Movement	Direction
&25	Hop back slightly, landing on left foot . . . then right (feet apart)	⇩
&26	Hop back slightly, landing on left foot . . . then right foot beside left (feet together)	
&27	Repeat steps &25	
&28	Repeat steps &26	
29	Step right foot forward	
30	Cross left foot over right	❍
31	Step right foot back	
32	Step on left, turning quarter turn left	◖

Begin again!

☆☆☆ Tropicana Parking Lot ☆☆☆

Patrick W. Riley, USA — ***Four Wall***

Beats	Movement	Direction
	Tropicana Shuffle	
	(Syncopation steps in place)	
1	Touch right toe to right side	❍
&	Step right foot beside left	
2	Touch left heel forward	
&	Step left foot beside right	
3	Touch right heel forward	
&	Step right foot beside left	
4	Touch left toe to left side	
&	Step left foot beside right	
5	Touch right heel forward	
&	Step right foot beside left	
6	Touch left heel forward	
&	Step left foot beside right	
7	Touch right toe to right side	
&	Step right foot beside left	
8	Touch left toe to left side	
&	Step left foot beside right	

Beats	Movement	Direction
	Heel-Ball-Cross (x2) Travelling Right	
	The next 16 counts (steps 9–24) are side movements with the body direction forward.	
9	Touch right heel forward	⇨

(Contd.)

Beats	Movement	Direction
&	Step right foot beside left on ball of foot	⇨
10	Cross left foot over right	
11&12	Repeat steps 9&10	
	Brush, Cross and Cross and Cross (Travelling Left)	
13	Brush right foot forward	⇦
14	Cross right foot over left	
&	Step left foot to left side	
15&	Repeat steps 14&	
16	Cross right foot over left	
	Heel-Ball-Cross (x2)	
17	Touch left heel forward	⇦
&	Step left foot beside right on ball of foot	
18	Cross right foot over left	
19&20	Repeat steps 17&18	
	Brush, Cross and Cross and Cross	
21	Brush left foot forward	⇨
22	Cross left foot over right	
&	Step right foot to right side	
23&	Repeat steps 22&	
24	Cross left foot over right	
	Toy Soldier (step forward and quarter pivot left 4 times)	

Beats	Movement	Direction
25	Touch right toe forward	
26	Pivot quarter turn left on ball of left foot	
27–32	Repeat steps 25,26 three more times *(you have completed 1 full turn, 360 degrees, counter-clockwise)*	

Walk Forward, Together, Walk Backward, Together

Beats	Movement	Direction
33–35	Walk forward, right, left, right	
36	Step left foot beside right	
37–39	Walk back, right, left, right	
40	Step left foot beside right	

Knees, Knees, Roll and Roll

Keep your knees and feet close together.

Beats	Movement	Direction
41	Bend knees forward-right at 45 degrees	
&	Return knees to centre	
42	Bend both knees forward-left at 45 degrees	
&	Return knees to centre	
43,44	Circle knees to left (counter-clockwise) twice	

Right Vine and Touch

Beats	Movement	Direction
45,46	Step right foot to right side. Step left foot behind right	

(Contd.)

Beats	Movement	Direction
47,48	Step right foot to right side. Touch left toe beside right	
	Left Vine	
49,50	Step left foot to left side. Step right foot behind left	
51,52	Step left foot turning quarter turn left. Touch right toe beside left	
53,54	Touch right toe forward. Pivot half turn left	
55,56	Repeat steps 53,54	

Begin again!

☆☆☆☆☆☆ Tush Push ☆☆☆☆☆☆

Four Wall

Although usually attributed to Jim Ferranzzano, there are many variations of this classic dance (especially on the first 8 counts). Watch out for the ones you like and adapt them for yourself.

Beats	Movement	Direction
	First 8 Counts	
	St Louis style	
1–4	Tap right heel forward 4 times	❍
&	Switch weight *(hop)* to right foot	
5–8	Tap left heel forward 4 times	
	OR	
1	Touch right heel forward	❍
2	Step right foot beside left	
3	Touch left heel forward	
4	Step left foot in place	
5–8	Repeat steps 1–4	
	OR	
1	Touch right heel forward	❍
2	Touch right foot beside left *(no weight change)*	
3,4	Touch right heel forward, tap twice	
&	Switch weight, return right foot to place	
5	Touch left heel forward	

(Contd.)

Beats	Movement	Direction
6	Touch left foot beside right *(no weight change)*	❍
7,8	Touch left heel forward, tap twice	
	These are just some of the variations, the third one seems to be the most popular.	
	Fast Heel Touches	
9	Touch right heel forward	❍
10	Step right foot back and touch left heel forward *(hop)*	
11	Step left foot back and touch right heel forward *(another hop)*	
12	Leave right heel forward and clap	
	Tush Push	
13&14	Push hips forward twice	❍
15&16	Push hips *(tush)* back twice	
17,18	Push hips forward. Push hips *(tush)* back	
19,20	Repeat steps 17,18 *(Steps 17–20 may be replaced with rolls or grinds etc.)*	
	Shuffle Forward and Rock	
21&22	Shuffle forward, right, left, right	⇧
23	Rock forward onto left foot	
24	Rock back onto right foot	

Beats	Movement	Direction
	Shuffle Backwards and Rock	
25&26	Shuffle back, left, right, left	⇩
27	Rock back onto right foot	
28	Rock forward onto left foot	
	Shuffle Forward Half Turn (x2)	
29&30	Shuffle forward, right, left, right	⇧
31	Step left foot forward	
32	Pivot half turn right	◗
33&34	Shuffle forward, left, right, left	⇧
35	Step right foot forward	
36	Pivot half turn left	◖
	Quarter Turn	
37	Step right foot forward	
38	Pivot quarter turn left, transferring weight to left foot	◤
39	Stomp right foot in place	
40	Clap (transfer weight to left foot)	○

Begin again!

☆☆☆☆☆ Vancouver Boogie ☆☆☆☆☆

Bill Bader, Vancouver, Canada — ***Four Wall***

Beats	Movement	Direction
	Right Vine	
1	Step right foot to right	⇨
2	Cross left foot behind right	
3	Step right foot to right	
4	Touch left heel diagonally forward left and clap	
	Left Vine	
5	Step left foot to left	⇦
6	Cross right foot behind left	
7	Step left foot to left	
8	Touch right heel diagonally forward right and clap	
	Diagonal Heel Touches	
9	Step right foot beside left	○
10	Touch left heel diagonally forward left and clap	
11	Step left foot beside right	
12	Touch right heel diagonally forward right and clap	

Beats	Movement	Direction
	Twists	
13	Step right foot beside left and swivel both heels to right	❍
14	Swivel both heels to left	
15	Swivel both heels to right	
16	Swivel both heels to centre	
	Stomps and Kicks	
17–18	Stomp right heel beside left twice *(do not shift weight to right foot)*	❍
19–20	Kick right foot forward twice	
	Ball-Change	
&	Step right toe next to left foot	❍
21	Step left foot in place	
	Stomps and Kicks	
22	Stomp right heel beside left	❍
23–24	Kick right foot forward twice	
	Hook, Hitch, Rock, Hitch and Turn	
25	Step right foot forward	❍
26	Raise left foot crossed behind right knee	
27	Step left foot back	
28	Raise *(hitch)* right knee	

(Contd.)

Beats	Movement	Direction
29	Step right foot back	❍
30	Rock forward onto left	
31	Scuff right heel forward	
32	Raise *(hitch)* right knee and make quarter turn to left, pivoting on ball of left foot	◖

Begin again!

☆☆☆☆☆ Walkin' the Line ☆☆☆☆☆

Four Wall

This version of 'Walking the Line' seems originally to have been 'Walk the Line' by Sandi Larkin, USA. In the original the dance begins at step 17, the quarter turn right on step 10 does not exist and there is a quarter turn right on step 12 (not a half turn), making 'Walk the Line' a four-wall dance, counter-clockwise.

Beats	Movement	Direction
	Double Kick, Shuffle Backwards, Cross and Touch	
1,2	Kick right foot forward twice	
3&4	Shuffle back right, left, right	
5	Cross left foot forward over right	
6	Point right toe to right side	
7	Cross right foot forward over left	
8	Step left foot to left side	
	Cross, Turn, Step, Turn	
9	Cross right foot behind left	
10	Swivel on ball of right foot, turning quarter turn right, touch left toe back	
11	Step left foot forward	
12	Swivel on ball of left foot, turning half turn left, step right foot back	

(Contd.)

Beats	Movement	Direction
	Shuffle Backwards, Rock, Shuffle Forward, Rock	
13&14	Shuffle back, left, right, left	⇩
15	Rock back onto right foot	❍
16	Rock forward onto left foot	
17&18	Shuffle forward, right, left, right	⇧
19&20	Shuffle forward, left, right, left	
21	Rock forward onto right foot	❍
22	Rock back onto left foot	
	Three Rolling Half Turns Clockwise	
23	On ball of left foot pivot half turn right, stepping right foot forward	◗
24	On ball of right foot pivot half turn right, stepping left foot back	◗
25	On ball of left foot pivot half turn right, stepping right foot forward	◗
26	Stomp left foot beside right	❍

Begin again!

☆☆☆☆ Waltz Across Texas ☆☆☆☆

Jim Ferrazzano, USA **One Wall**

This is a one-wall dance, meaning you will always begin again facing the same wall. There are many variations, including fewer twinkles or fewer moves forward or back. If this dance is done at your local club, then you may want to adjust accordingly.

Beats	Movement	Direction
	Twinkles	
1	Step left foot over right foot	❍
2	Step right foot to right of left foot	
3	Step left foot in place	
4	Step right foot over left foot	❍
5	Step left foot to left of right foot	
6	Step right foot in place	
7	Step left foot over right foot	❍
8	Step right foot to right of left foot	
9	Step left foot in place	
10	Step right foot over left foot	❍
11	Step left foot to left of right foot	
12	Step right foot in place	
	Move Forward	
13	Left step forward	⇧

(Contd.)

Beats	Movement	Direction
14	Right step forward	⇧
15	Left step forward	
16	Right step forward	⇧
17	Left step forward	
18	Right step forward	
	Move Back	
19	Left step back	⇩
20	Right step back	
21	Left step back	
22	Right step back	⇩
23	Left step back	
24	Right step back	
	Move Left	
25	Step left, placing your foot to begin a turn to left	⇦ ●
26	Step with right foot and pivot a full turn	
27	Step left, finishing the turn to come back facing original wall	
28	Cross in front with right foot	⇦
29	Step left	
30	Cross in back with right foot	

Beats	Movement	Direction
31	Step left	⇦
32	Rock right	○
33	Rock left	
	Move Right	
34	Step right, placing your foot to begin turn to right	● ⇨
35	Step with left foot and pivot a full turn to right	
36	Step right, finishing turn to come back facing original wall	
37	Cross in front with left foot	⇨
38	Step right	
39	Cross in back with left foot	
40	Step right	⇨
41	Rock left	
42	Rock right	
	Move Forward with Turn	
43	Step left with half turn to left	◖
44	Step back right	⇩
45	Step back left	
46	Step back right	⇩
47	Step back left	
48	Step back right	

(Contd.)

Beats	Movement	Direction
	Move Back with Turn	
49	Step left with half turn to left	◖
50	Step back right	⇩
51	Step back left	
52	Step back right	⇩
53	Step back left	
54	Step back right	

Begin again!

☆☆☆☆☆☆ 'X'ed Out ☆☆☆☆☆☆☆

Scott Lanius, Nashville, USA — ***Four Wall***

Beats	Movement	Direction
	Diagonal Steps and Touches	
1	Step right foot diagonally forward	⇗
2	Touch left foot beside right, snap fingers	
3	Step left foot back to place	⇙
4	Touch right foot beside left, clap	
5	Step right foot diagonally back	⇘
6	Touch left foot beside right, snap fingers	
7	Step left forward, turning half turn left	◖
8	Touch right foot beside left, clap	
9–15	Repeat steps 1–7	
16	Touch right toe to right side, clap	
	Cross and Touch	
17	Cross right foot over left	⇧
18	Touch left toe to left side	
19	Cross left foot over right	
20	Step right foot back	⇩
	Reverse Pivot, Forward Pivot	
21	Step left foot back	⇩
22	Pivot half turn left (on balls of both feet)	◖

(Contd.)

Beats	Movement	Direction
23	Step right foot forward	⇧
24	Pivot half turn left (on balls of both feet)	◖
	Sashay Left, Right, Left, Right to form a Square	
25	Step right foot to right side	⇨
&	Step left foot beside right	
26	Step right foot to right side	
&	Hitch left, turning quarter turn right	◗
27	Step left foot to left side	⇦
&	Step right foot beside left	
28	Step left foot to left side	
&	Hitch right, turning quarter turn right	◗
29	Step right foot to right side	⇨
&	Step left foot beside right	
30	Step right foot to right side	
&	Hitch left, turning quarter turn right	◗
31	Step left foot to left side	⇦
&	Step right foot beside left	
32	Step left foot to left side	

Begin again!

Advanced Level Dances

☆☆☆☆☆

☆☆☆☆ Achy Breaky Heart ☆☆☆☆

Melanie Greenwood, USA — ***Four Wall***

Beats	Movement	Direction
	Right Vine and Hip Sways	
1	Step right foot to right side	⇨
2	Step left foot behind right	
3	Step right foot to right side	
4	Hold	○
5	Sway hips left	
6	Sway hips right	
7	Sway hips left	
8	Hold *(weight on left foot)*	
	Star, Unwinding Turn and Hitch	
9	Touch right toe directly behind	○
10	Touch right toe out to right side	
11	Cross right foot over left	
12	Unwind three-quarter turn to left	◕
13	Step left foot back	⇩
14	Step right foot back	
15	Hitch left foot *(raise knee)*, turning quarter turn left on right foot	◖
16	Step left foot down in place	
	Walk Back and Hip Sways	
17	Step right foot back	⇩

Beats	Movement	Direction
18	Step left foot back	
19	Stomp right foot *(feet shoulder-width apart)*	
20	Hold	
21	Sway hips left	
22	Sway hips right	
23	Sway hips left	
24	Hold	
	Turns and Right Vine	
25	Quarter turn right on right foot	
26	Stomp left foot beside right, clap	
27	Half turn left on left foot	
28	Stomp right foot beside left, clap	
29	Step right foot to right side	
30	Step left foot behind right	
31	Step right foot to right side	
32	Stomp left foot beside right, clap	

Begin again!

☆☆☆☆☆ Ain't Goin' Down ☆☆☆☆☆

Two Wall

Beats	Movement	Direction
1,2	Tap right heel forward twice	❍
3,4	Tap right toe behind twice	
5	Tap right heel forward	
6	Tap right toe back	
7	Tap right heel forward	
8	Tap right toe back	
9	Stomp right foot home	❍
10	Touch left toe out to left	
11	Step left foot back home	
12	Stomp right foot	
13	Touch left toe out to left	
14	Step left foot home	
15	Touch right toe out to right	
16	Step right foot home	
17	Step back on left foot	❍
18	Extend right heel forward	
19	Step down on right foot	
20	Touch left foot next to right	

The next four steps are the same as above but twice as fast

Beats	Movement	Direction
21	Hop back on left foot and extend right heel forward at same time	○
22	Bring both feet back home	
23	Hop back on left foot and extend right heel forward at same time	
24	Bring both feet back home	
25	Touch left toe forward	
26	Turn quarter turn to right	◗
27	Stomp left foot	
28	Stomp right foot	○
29	Touch forward with left foot	
30	Turn quarter turn to right *(you will now be facing the opposite wall from which you started)*	◗
31	Stomp left foot	
32	Stomp right foot	
	Going on a Left Diagonal	
33	Step left	⇖
34	Drag right	
35	Step left	
36	Drag right	
	Right Vine	
37	Step right	⇨
38	Step behind right with left foot	

(Contd.)

Beats	Movement	Direction
39	Step right	
40	Scuff left	
	Left Vine	
41	Step left	
42	Step behind left with right foot	
43	Step left	
44	Stomp right, but don't put weight on it	
	Pivots	
45	Touch forward with right foot	
46	Turn half turn to left, pushing off of right foot	
47	Touch forward with right foot	
48	Turn half turn to left *After you finish the second turn, bring your right leg straight through to begin again with a double heel in front*	

Begin again!

☆☆☆☆☆☆ Apple Jack ☆☆☆☆☆☆

Four Wall

The first 8 counts are continuous weight transfers with double-time toe-heel swivels. The numbers in the dance description represent the one beat of music and the '&' symbol represents the down beat. It takes a lot of practice, so stick with it!

Beats	Movement	Direction
	Starting Position: Feet shoulder-width apart, weight on left heel and right toes.	
1	Swivel left toes to left and right heel to left *(feet are in a V position with the toes pointing out)*	❍
&	Swivel left toes and right heel back to centre *(as you come back to centre, transfer weight to left toes and right heel)*	
2	Swivel right toes to right and left heel to right *(feet are in a V position with toes pointing out)*	
&	Swivel right toes and left heel back to centre *(as you come back to centre, transfer weight to left heel and right toes)*	
3	Swivel left toes to left and right heel to left *(feet are in V position with toes pointing out)*	

(Contd.)

Beats	Movement	Direction
&	Swivel left toes back to centre and right heel back to centre *(keep weight balance the same)*	❍
4	Swivel left toes to left and right heel to left *(feet are in V position with toes pointing out)*	
&	Swivel left toes and right heel back to centre *(as you come back to centre, transfer weight to left toes and right heel)*	
5	Swivel right toes to right and left heel to right *(feet are in V position with toes pointing out)*	
&	Swivel right toes back to centre and left heel back to centre *(keep weight balance the same)*	
6	Swivel right toes to right and left heel to right *(feet are in V position with toes pointing out)*	
&	Swivel right toes and left heel back to centre *(as you come back to centre, transfer weight to left heel and right toes)*	
7	Swivel left toes to left and right heel to left *(feet are in V position with toes pointing out)*	
&	Swivel left toes and right heel back to centre *(as you come back to centre, transfer weight to left toes and right heel)*	

Beats	Movement	Direction
8	Swivel right toes to right and left heel to right *(feet are in V position with toes pointing out)*	❍
&	Swivel right toes back to centre and left heel back to centre *(transfer weight to left foot)*	
9	Right toe touch forward	❍
10	Right toe touch back	
11	Right step forward, turning a quarter turn to right	◗
12	Left foot touch to the left side	❍
13	Left cross-step over right foot	
14	Right foot touch to the right side	
15	Right cross-step over left foot	
16	Left step back	
17	Right step back next to left foot	
18	Jump forward with both feet *(shoulder-width apart to start the toe-heel twists again)*	⇧

Begin again!

Teach Yourself Applejack in 10 Easy Steps

1 Learn the 2nd part first . . . steps 9–18

2 Sit down, spread feet apart

3 Understand the dance; Applejacks are

(Contd.)

Beats	Movement	Direction
	done in two directions – left and right. Once you have mastered 1&2& you've got it!	
	Applejack Left:	
4	Fan left toes out, fan left toes centre *(weight on heel)*	❍
5	Fan right heel in, fan right heel centre *(weight on ball)*	
6	Try 4&5 together	
	Applejack Right:	
7	Fan right toes out, fan right toes centre *(weight on heel)*	❍
8	Fan left heel in, fan left heel centre *(weight on ball)*	
9	Try 7&8 together	
10	Now try: One left 1& One right 2& Two left 3&4& Two right 5&6& One left 7& One right 8&	

Now stand up and try it. Good luck!

☆☆☆☆☆☆☆ Arlene ☆☆☆☆☆☆☆

George Davis, Antioch, USA — ***Four Wall***

Beats	Movement	Direction
	Left Vine and Stomp	
1,2	Step left foot to left side. Step right foot behind left	⇦
3,4	Step left foot to left side. Step right foot over *(in front of)* left foot	
5	Step left foot to left side	
6	Stomp *(up)* right foot beside left ***(bring right foot back up, leaving weight on left)***	○
7	Stomp-up right foot beside left	
8	Stomp-up right foot beside left	
	Step Pivots	
9	Step right foot forward ***(leave left foot and leg extended behind, with ball of left foot still on the floor, but no weight on it)***	
10	Pivot half turn left on ball of right foot while transferring weight to left foot as you complete the pivot ***(leave right foot and leg extended behind you with the ball of your right foot still on the floor, but without weight on it)***	◖
11–16	Repeat steps 9,10 three more times	

Beats	Movement	Direction
	Heel, Hook, Heel, Together, Kick, Kick	
17	Touch right heel forward	❍
18	Cross right heel over left shin	
19	Touch right heel forward	
20	Step right foot beside left	
21,22	Kick left foot forward twice	
	Walk Backwards, Stomp, Touch, Stomp	
23–25	Walk back, left, right, left	⇩
26	Stomp right foot forward	
27	Touch right toe beside left instep	❍
28	Stomp right foot forward *(right heel approximately horizontal with left toe)*	
	'Louie, Louie'	
29	Swivel both heels in toward each other, weight on balls of both feet. Legs should look 'bowlegged' and toes pointed in opposite directions	❍
30	Swivel both heels out, away from each other so that both feet are now facing forward *(keep weight on balls of both feet in this move)*	
	Kick Down	
31	Kick right foot forward	

Beats	Movement	Direction
32	Step right foot down but forward *(right heel approximately horizontal with left toe)*	
	'Louie, Louie'	
33,34	Repeat steps 29,30	
	'Wooly Bully'	
35	Kick right foot forward	○
36	Hook right heel over left shin	
37	Pivot half turn left on ball of left foot, bring right foot back beside left knee *(right knee is bent during this entire move)*	◖
38	Step right foot back	
39	Scoot forward on right foot *(bend left knee)*	
40	Step left foot forward	
41	Bring right foot forward and hook right heel over left shin	
42	Pivot half turn left on ball of left foot, bring right foot back beside left knee *(right knee is bent during this entire move)*	◖
43	Step right foot back	
44	Scoot forward with right *(bend left knee)*	
	Rock, Rock, Turn, Stomp	
45	Rock forward onto left foot, leave	○

(Contd.)

Beats	Movement	Direction
	right foot and leg extended behind with ball of foot still on floor	
46	Rock back onto right foot, leave left leg extended forward with left foot slightly off the floor	
47	Step left foot forward, turning quarter turn left	
48	Stomp right foot beside left	

Heel Splits

Beats	Movement	Direction
49	Weight on balls of feet, split heels apart	
50	Bring heels together	
51,52	Repeat steps 49,50	

Monterey Turns

Beats	Movement	Direction
53	Touch right toe to right side	
54	Pivot half turn right on ball of left foot, bringing right foot around step right foot beside left completing turn	
55	Touch left toe to left side	
56	Step left foot beside right	
57–60	Repeat steps 53–56	

Hitch-Hike

Beats	Movement	Direction
61	Touch right toe diagonally back right 45 degrees. Hitch-hike right thumb back	

Beats	Movement	Direction
62	Step right foot back at 6 o'clock. Hitch-hike right thumb forward	⇩
63	Touch left toe diagonally back left 45 degrees. Move right thumb and forearm to left across stomach	
64	Step left foot back at 6 o'clock. Arm remains over stomach	
65–68	Repeat steps 61–64	
69	Repeat steps 61	
70	Weight on ball of left foot, pull right foot behind left, turning half turn right *(end with weight on right)* *Hands back to country-western position*	◗

Heel, Hook, Heel, Touch Back

Beats	Movement	Direction
71	Touch left heel forward	○
72	Hook left heel over right shin	
73	Touch left heel forward	
74	Touch left toe straight back	

Shoulder Shimmy

Beats	Movement	Direction
75	Step left foot forward, bend knees and drop down slightly. Shimmy shoulders and upper body	
76	Bring body back up continue to shimmy *(right leg is still extended back)*	
77	Step right foot beside left	

(Contd.)

Beats	Movement	Direction
78	Clap hands	
79	Step right foot back, bend knees and drop down slightly, shimmy shoulders and upper body	⇩
80	Bring body back up, continue to shimmy	
81	Step left foot back beside right	
82	Clap hands	
83–90	Repeat steps 75–82	

Begin again!

☆☆☆☆ Back in Your Arms ☆☆☆☆

Cathy Ryan (TCRG), Dublin, Ireland **Two Wall**

Beats	Movement	Direction
	Sailor Shuffle Going Backwards	
1&2	Right, left, right	
3&4	Left, right, left	
5&6	Right, left, right	
7&8	Left, right, left	
	Right Shuffle Forward, Step Half Turn, Left Shuffle, Step Hold	
9&10	Right shuffle forward *(right, left, right)*	
11,12	Step left, pivot half turn right	
13&14	Left shuffle forward *(left, right, left)*	
15,16	Step right foot forward, hold	
	Swivel Half Turn Hold, Two Half Turns, Quarter Paddle (or Chug) Turn	
17,18	Swivel toes half turn left, hold weight on left	
19,20	Step right, foot forward, pivot half turn left to back wall	
21,22	Step right, foot forward, pivot half turn left to front wall	
&23	Paddle (or chug) quarter turn to left	
&24	wall *(right, left, right, left)*	

(Contd.)

Beats	Movement	Direction
	Forward Half Turns, using Step Touches and Finger Clicks	
25,26	Step right to right side, swing left foot forward half turn to touch to right wall, snap fingers at shoulder level	⇧ ◗
27,28	Step left to left side, swing right foot forward half turn to touch to left wall, snap fingers at hip level	◖
29,30	Step right to right side, swing left foot forward half turn to touch to right wall, snap fingers at shoulder level	◗
31,32	Step left half turn left, step right beside left *(weight on the right)*	◖
	Sashay (Gallop) to Back Wall, Scissors	
33&34&	Sashey (gallop) left, right, left, right,	⇦ ◖
35&36	left, right, left *(4th beat, face back wall)*	
&37	Scissors: step right, cross left in front,	❍
&38	step right, left heel to left side	
&39	Scissors: step left, cross right in front,	
&40	step left, right heel to right side	
	Right Vine with Double Beats, 3 Mexican Heels, 2 Claps	
41,42	Vine right to right side, left behind	⇨
&43	Step right, left in front	
&44	Step right, left behind *(double time)*	

Beats	Movement	Direction
&45&	Heel switches: step right, left heel,	◌
46&47	step left, right heel, step right, left heel	
&48	Double clap while holding left heel	

Left Vine With Double Beats, 3 Mexican Heels, 2 Claps

Beats	Movement	Direction
49,50	Vine left to left side, right behind	⇦
&51	Step left, right in front	
&52	Step left, right behind *(double time)*	
&53&	Heel switches: step left, right heel,	◌
54&55	step right, left heel, step left, right heel	
&56	Double clap while holding right heel	

Begin again!

☆☆☆☆☆☆☆☆☆ Chaos ☆☆☆☆☆☆☆☆☆

Knox Rhine, Everett, USA **_Four Wall_**

Here is a collection of unique foot patterns that have emerged over the years and which have been put together to create Chaos. Thanks to all the choreographers for their time and talents.

Beats	Movement	Direction
	Steps 1–16	
	'Hawaiian Hustle' by Sue Shotwell	
	(16 beats)	
1	Kick right foot forward	❍
&	Step down on right toe, lifting left foot slightly	
2	Step down on left foot	
3	Kick right foot forward	
&	Step down on right toe, lift left foot slightly	
4	Step down on left foot	
5	Cross right foot over left and touching right toe down *(bend both knees and crouch down)*	
6	Pivot half turn to the left on the balls of both feet *(stand up straight)*	◖
7	Set both heels on floor	
8	Pause for 1 beat	
9–16	Repeat steps 1–8	

Beats	Movement	Direction
	Steps 17–32	
	'Hot Tamales' by Neal Hale	
	(16 beats)	
1	Step to right side with right foot. Push right shoulder forward, starting a slow quarter turn to left	
2–8	Stay on balls of both feet and continue pushing right shoulder forward. Straighten legs with weight on right foot after completion of turn	
1	Step to left side with left foot	⇦
2	Step across behind left leg with right	
3	Step a quarter turn left to left side with left foot	
4	Hop quarter turn to left, land with feet together	
5	Swivel heels to right side	⇨
6	Swivel toes to right side	
7	Swivel heels to right side	
8	Swivel toes to centre *(weight to right foot)*	

Beats	Movement	Direction
	Steps 33–44	
	'Arlene' by George Davis *(12 beats)*	
1	Walk back with left foot	⇩
2	Step back with right foot	
3	Step back with left foot	
4	Stomp right foot forward	

(Contd.)

Beats	Movement	Direction
5	Touch right toe next to left foot	
6	Stomp right foot forward	
7	Swivel both heels in	❍
8	Swivel both heels out	
1	Kick right foot forward	
2	Stomp right foot forward	
3	Swivel both heels in	
4	Swivel both heels out	

Steps 45–60

'Honky Tonk Twist' by Max Perry

(16 beats)

Beats	Movement	Direction
1	Step to left side with left foot	⇦
2	Step across behind left leg with right foot	
3	Step to left side with left foot	
4	Stomp-up with right foot	
5	Step to right side with right foot	⇨
6	Step across behind right leg with left foot	
7	Step to right side with right foot	
8	Stomp-down with left foot	
1	Split swivel to left	❍
2	Swivel centre	
3	Split swivel left	
4	Swivel centre	
5	Split swivel to right	

Beats	Movement	Direction
6	Swivel centre	
7	Split swivel right	
8	Swivel centre	

Steps 61–68
'God Blessed Texas' by Shirley K. Batson *(8 beats)*

Beats	Movement	Direction
1	Step forward with right foot	⇧
2	Kick left foot forward	
3	Torque turn half turn to right on ball of right foot and kick up left heel behind back	◗
4	Step forward with left foot	⇧
5	Lift right knee and scoot forward with left foot	
6	Keep right knee up and scoot on left foot again	
7	Step forward with right foot	
8	Lift left knee and scoot forward with right foot	

Steps 69–80
'Lost in Texas' by Jim Williams
(12 beats)

Beats	Movement	Direction
1	Step forward with left foot	
2	Stomp-up right foot next to left foot	
3	Step back with right foot	

(Contd.)

Beats	Movement	Direction
4	Place left foot next to right foot	
5	Place weight on ball of left foot and heel of right foot, swivel right toe to right and left heel to left. 'Hitch-hike' right thumb to right	❍
6	Swivel both feet back to centre. Bring thumb back to belt buckle	
7	Place weight on ball of left foot and heel of right foot, swivel right toe to right and left heel to left. 'Hitch-hike' right thumb to right	
8	Swivel both feet back to centre. Bring thumb back to belt buckle	
1	Step quarter turn right with left foot	
2	Pause	
3	Place right foot next to left foot	
4	Pause	

Steps 81–88
'Tropicana Parking Lot' by
Pat Riley
(8 beats)

Beats	Movement	Direction
1	Touch right toe to right side	❍
&	Place right foot next to left foot	
2	Touch left heel forward	
&	Place left foot next to right foot	
3	Touch right heel forward	

Beats	Movement	Direction
&	Place right foot next to left foot	
4	Touch left toe to left side	
&	Place left foot next to right foot	
5	Touch right heel forward	
&	Place right foot next to left foot	
6	Touch left heel forward	
&	Place left foot next to right foot	
7	Touch right toe to right side	
&	Place right foot next to left foot	
8	Touch left toe to left side	
&	Place left foot next to right foot	
	Steps 89–96	
	***'Thin Sole Shoes' by Susie Hollingsworth** (8 beats)*	
1	Step across left leg with right toe	
2	Set right heel down	
3	Step to left side with left toe	
4	Set left toe down	
5	Cross right foot in front of left leg	
	Begin quarter turn left	◀
6	Step back with left, completing turn	
7	Step forward with right foot	
8	Touch left toe next to right foot	
	Steps 97–108	
	'Dance Ranch Romp' by Jo Thompson	

(Contd.)

Beats	Movement	Direction
	(12 beats)	
&	Step back-left with left toe	❍
1	Touch right heel forward-right	
&	Step together with right foot	
2	Touch left toe next to right foot	
&	Step back-left with left toe	
3	Touch right heel forward-right	
&	Step together with right foot	
4	Touch left toe next to right foot	
5	Step to left side with left foot	
6	Step across behind left leg with right foot	⇦
7	Step to left side with left foot	
8	Touch right toe next to left foot	
&	Step back-right with right toe	❍
1	Touch left heel forward-left	
&	Step together with left foot	
2	Touch right toe next to left foot	
&	Step back-right with right toe	
3	Touch left heel forward-left	
&	Step together with left toe	
4	Touch right toe next to left foot	

Steps 109–116
'Heading South' by Ganean De la Grange *(8 beats)*

Beats	Movement	Direction
1	Touch right toe out to right side	

Beats	Movement	Direction
2	Slide right toe next to left foot and pivot quarter turn to right on ball of left foot, transfer weight to right foot after turn	◗
3	Touch left toe out to left side	
4	Slide left toe towards right foot and pivot half turn to left on ball of right foot, end with left toe crossed in front of right leg	◖
5	Step forward with left foot	
6	Lock/slide right foot forward behind left foot	⇧
7	Step forward with left foot	
8	Slide right toe forward next left foot	

Steps 117–128

***'Rodeo' by Dale White** (12 beats)*

Beats	Movement	Direction
1	Step forward with right foot	⇧
&	Slide left foot next to right foot	
2	Step forward with right foot	
&	Step forward with left foot	
3	Slide right foot next to left foot	
4	Step forward with left foot	
5	Cross right foot over left, making quarter turn left	◖
&	Step to left side with left foot	⇦
6	Cross right foot over left	

(Contd.)

Beats	Movement	Direction
&	Step to side with left	
7	Cross right foot over left	
&	Step to side with left	
8	Cross right foot over left	
&	Step to side with left	
1	Kick left foot forward	❍
2	Kick left foot forward	
3	Step behind right foot with left foot	
&	Step to side with right foot	
4	Step next to right with left foot	

Begin again!

☆☆☆☆ Charlie's Sidekick ☆☆☆☆

Charlie Milne, Canada **Four Wall**

This dance is challenging because of the many direction changes. After completion of one set (32 counts) you should end up just quarter turn to the left of where you started.

Beats	Movement	Direction
	1st Direction Change	
	Right Vine	
1	Step right foot to right	⇨
2	Cross left foot behind right	
3	Step right foot into quarter turn to left	◖
4	Scuff left foot next to right	
	2nd Direction Change	
	Left Vine	
5	Step left foot to left	⇦
6	Cross right foot behind left	
7	Step left foot into quarter turn to right	◗
8	Scuff right foot next to left	
	3rd Direction Change	
	Right Vine	
9	Step right foot to right	⇨
10	Cross left foot behind right	
11	Step right foot back and to right of	

(Contd.)

Beats	Movement	Direction
	left foot into quarter turn to right	◗
12	Touch left toe next to right foot and clap	

	4th Direction Change	
	Left Vine	
13	Step left foot to left	⇦
14	Cross right foot behind left	
15	Step left foot to left	
16	Spin half turn to left with weight on ball of left foot and pushing off with right foot	◖

	Step-Ball-Change	
17	Step right foot forward	❍
&	Step on ball of left foot in place	
18	Step right foot in place	
19	Step left foot forward	
&	Step on ball of right foot in place	
20	Step left foot in place	

	Kicks	
21–22	Kick right foot forward twice	❍
23	Step back on right foot	
24	Touch left toe next to right foot and clap	

Beats	Movement	Direction
	5th & 6th Direction Changes	
	Side Kick	
25	Step left foot forward	
26	Kick right foot out to side as you make quarter turn to left, turning on ball of left foot	◖
27	Cross right foot over left	
28	Raise both heels and unwind in half turn to left	◖
	7th & 8th Direction Changes	
	Side Kick	
29	Step right foot forward	
30	Kick left foot out to side as you make quarter turn to right, turning on ball of right foot	◗
31	Cross left foot over right	
32	Raise both heels and unwind in half turn to left	◖

Begin again!

☆☆☆☆ Cowboy Hip-Hop ☆☆☆☆

One Wall

Beats	Movement	Direction
	Running Man	
	This first part is like skipping in place three times	
1	Step forward on right foot	❍
&	Slide right foot back, lifting left foot	
2	Step down and forward on left foot	
&	Slide left foot back, lifting right foot	
3	Step down and forward on right foot	
&	Slide right foot back, lifting left foot	
4	Step down and forward with left foot	
	Hip Rolls	
5	Step forward on right foot and roll hips forward	❍
6	Roll hips back toward left foot	
7	Roll hips forward	
8	Roll hips back *(ending with weight on*	

Beats	Movement	Direction
	left foot and right foot still forward)	
	Here you can take it easy...	
9	Step back with right foot	❍
10	Step in place with left foot	
11	Step forward with right foot	
12	Step in place with left foot	
	...because here you do the same thing but in double-time	
13	Step back with right foot	❍
&	Step in place with left foot	
14	Step forward with right foot	
&	Step in place with left foot	
15	Step back with right foot	
&	Step in place with left foot	
16	Step right foot next to left foot *(put weight on right foot)*	
	Left Vine	
17	Step to the left with your left foot	⇦
18	Step behind your left foot with your right foot	
19	Step farther to the left with your left	
20	Clap	
	Here is where you can be dramatic	
21	With right foot, take a BIG step to	⇨

(Contd.)

Beats	Movement	Direction
	the right, arms spread out	
22	Slide left foot to right side	⇨
23	Step in place with right foot	
24	Step in place with left foot	❍

Jumping Jacks

25	Jump out *(spread legs shoulder-width apart; spread arms too)*	
&	Jump in *(bring feet back together and arms back close to body)*	
26	Jump out	
&	Jump in AND do a half turn left *(its easier than it sounds)*	◖
27	Jump out	
&	Jump in	
28	Jump out	

Chug Turns

In this next part you will be doing four chugs with your right leg to bring you around a half turn to face where you began. Your legs are shoulder-width apart; keep weight on left foot

29	Touch right toes out slightly in front	
&	and do a 1/8 turn to left, pushing off with right foot	

Beats	Movement	Direction
30	Touch right toes out slightly in front	
&	and do a 1/8 turn to left, pushing off with right foot	
31	Touch right toes out slightly in front	
&	and do a 1/8 turn to left, pushing off with right foot	
32	Touch right toes out slightly in front	
&	and do a 1/8 turn to left, pushing off with right foot	

Begin again!

☆☆☆☆☆☆ Electric Reel ☆☆☆☆☆☆

Regina & Robert Padden, Castlebar, Ireland **Four Wall**

This is often danced to Cry of the Celts *from* The Lord of the Dance. Alternatively, *if danced to the traditional* Mason's Apron, *start on the 33rd beat and hand movements come in on the 3rd wall with the drums. For hand movements, extend both arms to the left at shoulder height during counts 9, 10. You can also move your hands from side to side at waist level to coincide with the applejack steps.*

Beats	Movement	Direction
	Chassé Right, Heel switches	
1&2	Step right foot to right side. Hold.	⇨
&3	Step left foot beside right. Step right foot to right side.	
&4	Step left foot beside right. Step right foot to right side.	
5–6	Touch left heel forward. Touch right heel forward.	❍
7–8	Touch left heel forward. Clap.	
	Chassé Left, Heel switches	
9–10	Step left foot to left side. Hold.	⇦
&11	Step right foot beside left. Step left foot to left side.	
&12	Step right foot beside left. Step left foot to left side.	
13–14	Touch right heel forward. Touch left heel forward.	❍

Beats	Movement	Direction
15	Touch left heel forward.	
&16	Step right foot beside left. Step left foot in place.	

Beats	Movement	Direction
	Applejacks	
17&18&	Applejack left, centre, right, centre.	
19&20	Applejack left, centre, right	

Beats	Movement	Direction
	Hitch, Shuffle, Scuff, Hitch, Step	
&	Hitch right foot across in front of left and scoot slightly forward on left foot.	
21&22	Shuffle forward (*right, left, right*).	
23	Scuff left foot forward.	
&	Hitch left foot across in front of right and scoot slightly forward on the right foot.	
24	Step forward on the left foot.	

Beats	Movement	Direction
	Hitch, Shuffle, Scuff, Three-quarter turn, Step Back	
&	Hitch right foot across in front of left and scoot slightly forward on left foot.	
25&26	Shuffle forward (*right, left, right*).	
27&	Scuff left foot forward. Pivot three-quarter turn right on ball of right foot	
28	Step back on the left foot.	

Beats	Movement	Direction
	Coaster Step, Hold, Jump	
29&30	Step back on right foot. Step left foot beside right. Step forward on right foot.	❍
31–32	Hold. Jump forward on both feet.	⇧

Begin again!

☆☆☆☆☆☆ Foot Loose ☆☆☆☆☆☆

Knox Rhine, Everett, USA — ***Four Wall***

Beats	Movement	Direction
	Tap-Tap-Tap, Behind-Side-In-Front	
	Lean forward right with taps	
1	Tap right toe forward – right	
&	Tap right toe farther forward – right	
2	Step right foot forward – right	
3	Step left foot behind right	⇨
&	Step right foot to right side	
4	Cross left foot over right	
	Slap, Step, Back-Lock-Back	
5	Swing right leg up behind left leg and slap with left hand	○
6	Step right foot back diagonally right	⬂
7	Step left foot back diagonally left	⬃
&	Step right foot back diagonally, locking in front of left foot	
8	Step left foot back diagonally left	
	Shuffle Forward, Three-quarter Turn Right	
9&10	Shuffle forward, right, left, right	⇧
11	Step left foot, turning quarter turn right *(3 o'clock)*	◗

(Contd.)

Beats	Movement	Direction
&	Step right foot, turning quarter turn right *(6 o'clock)*	◗
12	Step left foot, turning quarter turn right *(9 o'clock)*	◗
	Shuffle Backward, Rock	
13&14	Shuffle back, right, left, right	⇩
15	Step left foot back	
16	Rock forward onto right foot	
	Repeat steps 1–16 with left foot leading . . .	
	Tap-Tap-Tap, Behind-Side-In-Front	
	Lean forward left with taps	
17	Tap left toe forward – left	
&	Tap left toe farther forward – left	
18	Step left foot forward – left	
19	Step right foot behind left	⇦
&	Step left foot to left side	
20	Cross right foot over left	
	Slap, Step, Back-Lock-Back	
21	Swing left leg up behind right leg and slap with right hand	○
22	Step left foot back diagonally left	⬃
23	Step right foot back diagonally right	⬂
&	Step left foot back diagonally, locking	

Beats	Movement	Direction
	in front of right foot	
24	Step right foot back diagonally right	⇘
	Shuffle Forward, Three-quarter Turn Left	
25&26	Shuffle forward, left, right, left	⇧
27	Step right foot, turning quarter turn left *(6 o'clock)*	
&	Step left foot, turning quarter turn left *(3 o'clock)*	
28	Step right foot, turning quarter turn left *(12 o'clock)*	
	Shuffle Backwards, Rock	
29&30	Shuffle back, left, right, left	⇩
31	Step right foot back	
32	Rock forward onto left foot	
	Cross, Unwind, Heel-Toe-Cross	
33	Cross right foot over left *(ball of foot)*	
34	Unwind half turn left on balls of both feet	
35	Touch left heel across right to right side	
&	Step on ball of left foot beside right	
36	Cross right foot over left	

(Contd.)

Beats	Movement	Direction
	Re-Cross, Unwind, Heel-Toe-Cross	
37	Cross left foot over right *(ball of foot)*	
38	Unwind half turn right on balls of both feet	◗
39	Touch right heel across left to left side	
&	Step on ball of right foot beside left	
40	Cross left foot over right	
	Backwards Half Monterey	
41	Touch right toe to right side	
42	Pivot half turn left on ball of left foot, place right foot beside left	◖
43	Touch left toe to left side	
44	Step left foot beside right	
	Backwards Quarter Monterey	
45	Touch right toe to right side	
46	Pivot quarter turn left on ball of left foot, place right foot beside left	◤
47	Touch left toe to left side	
48	Step left foot beside right	
	Fan and Fan and Toes-Heels-Heels-Toes	
49	Fan right toe to right side	❍
&	Return right toe to centre	
50	Fan left toe to left side	

Beats	Movement	Direction
&	Return left toe to centre	
51	Fan both toes out	
&	Fan both heels out	
52	Fan both heels in	
&	Fan both toes in	
	Single Applejacks: L-R-L-R, Hook	
53	Fan left toe and right heel to left	
&	Fan left toe and right heel to centre	
54	Fan right toe and left heel to right	
&	Fan right toe and left heel to centre	
55	Fan left toe and right heel to left	
&	Fan left toe and right heel to centre	
56	Fan right toe and left heel to right	
&	Fan right toe centre and hook left heel over right shin	
	Diagonal Cha-Chas	
57&58	Shuffle forward left diagonal *(2 o'clock)*, left, right, left	
59&60	Shuffle forward right diagonal *(4 o'clock)*, right, left, right	
	Roger Rabbit's, Rock Step	
&	Scoot forward on right foot turning slightly left to face wall *(3 o'clock)*	
61	Step left foot behind right leg	

(Contd.)

Beats	Movement	Direction
&	Scoot forward on left foot	
62	Step right foot behind left leg	
&	Scoot forward on right foot	
63	Step left foot behind right leg	
&	Rock forward onto right foot	
64	Rock back onto left foot	

Begin again!

Author's Note:
I have added clock positions to the original step description to aid direction. They are true for 1st wall only.

☆ G.M.C. (Go Marissa & Courtney) ☆

Marissa Mason and Courtney Ozover **Four Wall**

Beats	Movement	Direction
	Kick, Kick, Triple-step	
1	Kick right foot forward	❍
2	Kick right foot to right side	
3&4	Triple-step in place, right, left, right	
5	Kick left foot forward	
6	Kick left foot to left side	
7&8	Triple-step in place, left, right, left	
	Sailor Shuffles	
9	Cross right foot behind left	⇩
&	Step left foot to left side	
10	Step right foot in place	
11	Cross left foot behind right	
&	Step right foot to right side	
12	Step left foot in place	
13,14	Stomp right foot beside left. Stomp left foot in place	❍
15,16	Clap hands twice	
	Kick-Ball-Change, Step, Half Turn	
17	Kick right foot forward	❍
&	Step on ball of right foot	
18	Step left foot in place	

(Contd.)

Beats	Movement	Direction
19&20	Repeat steps 17&18	❍
21	Step right foot forward	
22	Pivot half turn left	◖
23,24	Stomp left foot in place. Stomp right foot beside left	
	Heel Grinds Walking Forward	
25	Step right heel forward toes up and pointed inward	⇧
26	Grind heel by fanning toes outward then lower right foot to floor, taking full weight	
27	Step left heel forward toes up and pointed inward	
28	Grind heel by fanning toes outward then lower left foot to floor, taking full weight	
29–32	Repeat steps 25–28	
	Running Man	
33	Step right foot forward	❍
&	Scoot back on right foot, hitching left knee	
34	Step left foot forward	
&	Scoot back on left foot, hitching right knee	
35&36&	Repeat steps 33&34&	

Beats	Movement	Direction
	Shuffle Forward, Half Turn, Stomp, Clap	
37&38	Shuffle forward, right, left, right	⇧
39&40	Shuffle forward, left, right, left	
41	Step right foot forward	
42	Pivot half turn left	◖
43	Step left foot in place	
44	Stomp right foot beside left, clap	
	Right Heel Swivels	
&	Weight on left foot, lift right heel slightly off floor, swivel out to right	❍
45	Swivel right heel in (to centre)	
&46–48	Repeat &45 three more times	
	Mashed Potatoes (Charleston Swivels), travelling backwards	
&	Lift right foot slightly off floor, turning both toes in, heels out	⇩
49	Step back onto right foot, turning both toes out, heels in	
&	Lift left foot slightly off floor, turning both toes in, heels out	
50	Step back onto left foot, turning both toes out, heels in	
&	Lift right foot slightly off floor, turning both toes in, heels out	

(Contd.)

Beats	Movement	Direction
51	Step back onto right foot, turning both toes out, heels in	⇩
&52	Swivel both heels out. Swivel both heels in	❍
	Repeat 'Mashed Potatoes', travelling backwards with left foot leading . . .	
&	Lift left foot slightly off floor, turning both toes in, heels out	⇩
53	Step back onto left foot, turning both toes out, heels in	
&	Lift right foot slightly off floor, turning both toes in, heels out	
54	Step back onto right foot, turning both toes out, heels in	
&	Lift left foot slightly off floor, turning both toes in, heels out	
55	Step back onto left foot, turning both toes out, heels in	
&56	Swivel both heels out. Swivel both heels in	❍
	Jump, Clap, Jump, Jump, Clap	
57	Jump forward on both feet	⇧
58	Clap	
&59	Jump forward on both feet, twice	
60	Clap	

Beats	Movement	Direction
	Jazz Box Turning Quarter Left, Jump, Clap	
61	Cross right foot over left	○
62	Step left foot back, turning quarter left *(9 o'clock)*	◖
63	Step right foot to right side	
64	Jump forward on both feet, clap	

Begin again!

☆☆☆ The Honky Tonk Twist ☆☆☆

Max Perry, Danbury, USA **_Four Wall_**

Beats	Movement	Direction
	Heel Twists	
1	With weight on balls of feet, twist both heels to right	❍
2	Bring heels back to centre	
3	Twist both heels to right	
4	Bring heels back to centre	
5	Touch right heel forward	❍
6	Hook (cross) in front of left leg	
7	Touch right heel forward	
8	Bring right foot back next to left	
	Heel Twists	
9	With weight on balls of feet, twist both heels to left	❍
10	Bring heels back to centre	
11	Twist both heels to left	
12	Bring heels back to centre	
13	Touch left heel forward	
14	Hook (cross) in front of right leg	
15	Touch left heel forward	
16	Touch left foot back next to right	

Beats	Movement	Direction
	Charlestons	
17	Step forward on left	○
18	Kick right foot forward	
19	Step back on right foot	
20	Touch left toe back	
21	Step forward on left	○
22	Kick right foot forward	
23	Step back on right foot, turning quarter turn to right	
24	Touch left foot next to right	
	Left Vine	
25	Step to the left with left foot	⇦
26	Cross behind left with right foot	
27	Step to the left with left foot	
28	Stomp right foot and clap	
	Right Vine	
29	Step to the right with right foot	⇨
30	Cross behind right with left foot	
31	Step to the right with right foot	
32	Stomp left foot and clap	
	Swivet	
33	With weight on left heel and right toes, twist left toes and right heel to left	○

(Contd.)

Beats	Movement	Direction
34	Centre feet	
35	Twist to left *(same as step 33)*	O
36	Centre feet *(switch weight to right heel and left toes)*	
37	Twist right toes and left heel to right	
38	Centre feet	
39	Twist right toes and left heel to right *(same as step 37)*	
40	Centre feet	
	Slow Walk Back	
41	Step back with right toe	⇩
42	Bring right heel down and clap	
43	Step back with left toe	
44	Bring left heel down and clap	
45	Step back with right toe	
46	Bring right heel down and clap	
47	Step back with left toe	
48	Bring left heel down and clap	
	Forward Slides	
49	Step forward with right foot	⇧
50	Slide left foot up to right foot	
51	Step forward with right foot	
52	Scuff left foot past right foot	
53	Step forward with left foot	
54	Slide right foot up to left foot	

Beats	Movement	Direction
55	Step forward with left foot	
56	Scuff right foot past left foot	
	Drunken Sailor Walk	
57	Cross right foot over left foot	⇧
58	Hold	
59	Cross left foot over right foot	
60	Hold	
61	Cross right foot over left foot	
62	Hold	
63	Step left foot next to right foot	❍
64	Hold and clap	

Begin again!

☆☆☆☆☆☆ Hot Tamales ☆☆☆☆☆☆

Neil Hale, Pleasanton, USA — ***Two Wall***

Beats	Movement	Direction
	Right Kick-Ball-Change, Toe Struts	
1&	Kick right foot forward. Step right foot beside left on ball of foot	❍
2	Step left foot beside right	
3,4	Touch right toe forward. Lower right heel	⇧
5,6	Touch left toe beside right. Lower left heel	❍
	Monterey Turns, Hitch-Hike Swivel	
7,8	Point right toe to right side. Pivot half turn on ball of left foot, stepping right foot beside left	◗
9,10	Point left toe to left side. Step left front beside right	
11–14	Repeat steps 7–10 *(ending with weight on ball of left foot and heel of right foot)*	◗
15	Swivel right toe right. Swivel left heel left *(hitch-hike right thumb right)*	❍
16	Swivel right toe centre. Swivel left heel centre	

Beats	Movement	Direction
	Left Vine, Boot Slaps with Turn	
17,18	Step left foot to left side. Step right foot behind left	⇦
19,20	Step left foot to left side. Step right foot in place, taking weight on right	
21,22	Swing left foot behind right leg, slap left heel with right hand. Step left foot to left side	
23	Swing right foot in front of left leg, slap right heel with left hand	
24	Pivot quarter turn left, swinging right foot out to right side, slap right heel with right hand	
	'Hot Tamale' Shoulder Pushes	
25	Step right foot to right side *(feet apart, bend knees and crouch down).* Push right shoulder forward, starting shimmies as you start a slow quarter turn left	
26–32	With feet apart, weight on balls of feet, continue shoulder pushes (shimmies) until you have made quarter turn left as you straighten up *(end with weight on left foot)*	

(Contd.)

Beats	Movement	Direction
	Toe Struts, Finger Snaps	
33,34	Touch right toe back. Lower right heel, snap right fingers	
35,36	Touch left toe back. Lower left heel, snap left fingers	
37,38	Touch right toe back. Lower right heel, snap right fingers	
39,40	Touch left toe back. Hold left foot in position and snap left fingers	
	Left Vine with Half Turn, Swivels	
41,42	Step left foot to left side. Step right foot behind left	
43,44	Step left foot, turning quarter turn left. With feet together hop another quarter turn left	
45,46	Swivel heels right. Swivel toes right	
47,48	Swivel heels right. Swivel toes centre *(end with weight on right foot)*	
	Pivot, Step, Scoot, Step, Stomp, Clap	
49,50	Step left foot forward. Pivot half turn right *(change weight to right)*	
51,52	Step left foot forward. Scoot forward on left foot bringing right knee up	
53,54	Step right foot forward. Stomp left foot beside right	

Beats	Movement	Direction
55,56	Clap with right palm up and left down Clap with left palm up and right down	❍
	Knee Rolls	
57	Roll left knee to centre in front of right *(right leg is straight)*	❍
58	Roll left knee back to starting position	
59	Roll right knee to centre in front of left *(left leg is straight)*	
60	Roll right knee back to starting position	
	Knee Pops	
61&	Pop left knee to centre in front of right. Return left to starting position	❍
62&	Pop right knee to centre in front of left. Return right to starting position	
63&	Pop left knee to centre in front of right. Return left to starting position	
64	Pop right knee to centre in front of left, keep weight on left	
	Begin again!	

☆☆☆☆☆ Indian Runner ☆☆☆☆☆

Julie L. Weith, USA

Two Wall

Beats	Movement	Direction
&1	Step out to right on right, then step out to left on left	❍
&2	Touch right toe next to left, then touch right out to right	
3	Touch right toe next to left	
4	Step right to right	
&5	Step back on left, touch right heel forward	
&6	Step forward on right, then cross left over right	
7	Make half turn to right on balls of both feet *(unwind legs)*	◗
8	Clap	
9	Cross left over right	⇧
10	Kick right out to right	
11	Cross right over left	
12	Kick left out to left	
13	Cross left over right	
14	Hitch right knee while scooting back on left	⇩
15&16	Shuffle-step in place, right, left, right	❍

Beats	Movement	Direction
	Chassé Left, Rock Step	
17	Step left foot to left	⇦
&	Slide right foot next to left	
18	Step left foot to left	
19	Cross right foot behind left and rock back toward 8 o'clock, while hitching left knee	
20	Rock forward toward 2 o'clock on left foot	
	Chassé Right, Rock Step	
21	Step right foot to right	⇨
&	Slide left foot next to right	
22	Step right foot to right	
23	Cross left foot behind right and rock back toward 4 o'clock, while hitching right knee	
24	Rock forward toward 10 o'clock on right foot	
	Half Turns	
25	Step forward on left foot	
26	Make half turn to right, shifting weight to right foot	◗
27	Step forward on left foot	
28	Make half turn to right, shifting weight to right foot	◗

(Contd.)

Beats	Movement	Direction
29&30	Left shuffle-step forward *(left, right, left)*	⇧
31&32	Right shuffle-step forward *(right, left, right)*	
	Backward Skip	
33	Step back on left foot	⇩
&	Hitch right knee as you scoot back on left	
34	Step back on right foot	
&	Hitch left knee as you scoot back on right	
35	Step back on left	
&	Hitch right knee as you scoot back on left	
36	Stomp right foot next to left *(don't put weight on right foot)*	

Begin again!

☆☆☆☆☆☆ Kickin' It Up ☆☆☆☆☆☆

Scott Lanius, Nashville, USA — ***Two Wall***

Beats	Movement	Direction
	Kick-Ball-Point	
1	Kick right foot forward	○
&	Step on ball of right foot	
2	Point left toe out to left side	
3	Kick left foot forward	
&	Step on ball of left foot	
4	Point right foot out to right side	
5	Step right foot forward	
6	Scoop left foot forward	
7	Touch left foot back	
8	Pivot half turn left, switching weight to left foot	◖
	Pivot Turns	
9	Step right foot forward	
10	Pivot half turn left	◖
11	Step right foot forward	
12	Pivot three-quarter turn left	◕
	Side Triple and Unwind	
13&14	Triple-step to right side *(right, left, right)*	⇨
15	Cross left foot behind right	
16	Unwind half turn left	◖

(Contd.)

Beats	Movement	Direction
17–24	Repeat steps 1–8	
	Shuffle Forward	
25&26	Shuffle forward, right, left, right	⇧
27&28	Shuffle forward, left, right, left	
	Chug Turn Three-quarter Left	
29	Point right toe to right side	◕
&	Slight turn left on left foot	
30	Point right toe to right side	
&	Slight turn left on left foot	
31	Point right toe to right side	
&	Slight turn left on left foot	
32	Point right toe to right side	
&	Slight turn left on left foot	
	Begin again!	

☆☆☆☆☆☆ Kneel Hail ☆☆☆☆☆☆

Compiled by Rocks Nine as a tribute to Neil Hale **Four Wall**

Beats	Movement	Direction
	'Cruisin'	
	Figure 8 Vine	
1	Step left foot to left side	⇦
2	Step right foot behind left	
3	Step left foot forward, turning quarter turn left	
4	Step right foot forward	
5	Pivot half turn left	
6	Step right foot forward, turning quarter turn left *(face 12 o'clock)*	
7	Step left foot behind right	
8	Step right foot forward, turning quarter turn right	
9	Step left foot forward	
10	Pivot half turn right	
11	Step left foot forward, turning quarter turn right *(face 12 o'clock)*	
12	Rock to right side, shifting weight to right foot	○

'Hot Tamale'

Slap, Side, Slap, Quarter Turn

13 Swing left foot up behind right leg.

(Contd.)

Beats	Movement	Direction
	Slap with right hand	
14	Step left foot to left side	
15	Swing right foot up behind left leg. Slap with left hand	
16	Swing right foot out to right side, turning quarter turn left. Slap with right hand	◖
	Shoulder Push	
17	Step right foot to right side *(bend knees)*. Push right shoulder forward, starting a slow quarter turn left	◖
18–24	Stay on balls of both feet and continue pushing right shoulder forward. On completion of turn straighten legs, end with weight on left	
	'Cowboy Hand Jive' ***Shuffle, Quarter Turn, Shuffle***	
25&26	Shuffle forward, right, left, right	⇧
&	Pivot half turn left on ball of right foot	◖
27&28	Shuffle forward, left, right, left	⇧
	Quarter Turn, Shuffle, Half Turn, Shuffle	
&	Pivot quarter turn right on ball of left foot	◗

Beats	Movement	Direction
29&30	Shuffle forward, right, left, right	⇧
&	Pivot quarter turn left on ball of right foot	◖
31&32	Shuffle forward, left, right, left	⇧

'Linda Lu'
Out-Out, In-In, Out-Out, In-In
Travel backward on following steps . . .

Beats	Movement	Direction
&	Step right foot out to right side	⇩
33	Step left foot out to left side	
&	Step right foot to centre	
34	Step left foot to centre	
&35–36	Repeat steps &33&34 once more	

Wiggle Walks

Beats	Movement	Direction
37&38	Step right foot quarter turn left, bump hips right, left, right	◖
39	Pivot quarter turn right on ball of right foot	◗
40	Touch left toe beside right. Clap	○
41&42	Step left foot quarter turn right, bump hips left, right, left	◗
43	Pivot quarter turn left on ball of left foot	◖
44	Touch right toe beside left. Clap	
45&52	Repeat steps 37–44 once more	

(Contd.)

Beats	Movement	Direction
	'Cha-Cha Lengua'	
	Touch, Pivot, Turns	
53	Touch left toe forward	
54	Pivot half turn right on ball of right foot	◗
55	Pivot quarter turn right on ball of right foot, stepping left foot to left side	◥
&	Pivot quarter turn right on ball of left foot, stepping right foot to right side	◥
56	Step left foot back	

Beats	Movement	Direction
	Quarter Turn, In Front, Quarter Turn, Half Turn	
57	Pivot quarter turn right on ball of left foot, stepping right foot to right side	◥
58	Cross left foot over right	
59	Pivot quarter turn left on ball of left foot, stepping right foot back	◤
&	Hitch left knee high	
60	Pivot half turn left on ball of right foot	◖

Beats	Movement	Direction
	'Prancing Pony'	
	Step, Together, Paw, Paw	
61	Step left foot forward	○
62	Step right foot beside left	
63	Reverse scuff with ball of left foot	
64	Reverse scuff with ball of left foot	

Begin again!

☆☆☆☆☆ Le Doux Shuffle ☆☆☆☆☆

Four Wall

This looks a little like the Tush Push, but don't be fooled! It has more steps and is more strenuous.

Beats	Movement	Direction
1	Touch right heel forward	❍
2	Hook right heel *(cross right foot over left shin)*	
3	Touch right heel forward	
4	Step right foot back in place next to left	
5	Touch left heel forward	
6	Hook left heel *(cross left foot over right shin)*	
7	Touch left heel forward	
8	Step left foot back in place next to right	
9	Touch right heel forward	
10	Hook right heel	
11	Touch right heel forward	
12	Touch right toe back	

Shuffles and Turns

Beats	Movement	Direction
13&14	Right shuffle-step forward *(right, left, right)*	⇧
15	Step forward on left foot	

Beats	Movement	Direction
16	Rock back onto right foot in place	
17&18	Left shuffle-step back *(left, right, left)*	⇩
19	Step back with right foot	
20	Rock forward onto left foot in place	
21&22	Right shuffle-step forward	⇧
23	Step left foot forward	
24	Turn half turn to right, pushing off with left foot, pivoting on right foot	◗
25&26	Left shuffle-step forward	⇧
27	Touch right foot forward	
28	Turn quarter turn to left	◖
29	Touch right foot forward	
30	Turn half turn to left	◖
	Toe Taps	
31	Stomp right foot next to left	○
32	Clap	
33–36	Tap right toe 4 times *(with weight on left foot)*	
37–40	Hop and switch weight to right foot, tap left toe 4 times	
	This part is like the hops in the Tush Push	
41	Hop and switch weight, putting right heel forward	○
42	Hop and switch weight, putting left foot forward	

(Contd.)

Beats	Movement	Direction
43	Hop and switch weight, putting right foot forward	❍
44	Clap	
45,46	Bump right hip forward twice	
47,48	Bump left hip back twice	
49	Bump right hip forward	
50	Bump left hip backward	
51	Bump right hip forward	
52	Bump left hip backward	
53–70	Repeat Shuffles and Turns; steps 13–30	
	Jumping Jack Turn	
71	Stomp right foot next to left	❍
72	Jump in place, landing with feet spread shoulder-width apart	
73	Jump in place, landing with right foot crossed over left	
74	Turn half turn to left, with weight on left foot, unwinding legs	◖
75–92	Repeat Shuffles and Turns; steps 13–30	
	Jazz Box	
93	Step across left foot with right foot	❍
94	Step back on left foot	
95	Step back on right foot	
96	Stomp left foot next to right	

Begin again!

☆☆☆ Long-Legged Hannah ☆☆☆

Parry Spence, Nashville, USA — ***Four Wall***

Beats	Movement	Direction
	The Hitch-hiker	
1	With weight on right heel and ball of left foot, pivot right and throw your right thumb to right, like a hitch-hiker	❍
2	Pivot back to centre	
3	Repeat step 1	
4	Return feet to centre, then shift weight to ball of right foot and left heel	
5	Pivot left, throw left thumb out to left	
6	Return feet to centre	
7	Repeat step 5	
8	Return feet to centre	
	Clock Turn	
9	Step with right foot to right to 3 o'clock position, making a quarter turn	◔
10	Step with left foot across right to 6 o'clock, making another quarter turn	◔
11,12	Pivot half turn back to original wall. Clap *(end with right foot in front of left)*	◗
	Shoulder Rolls	
13,14	Roll left shoulder back slowly	❍
15,16	Roll right shoulder back slowly	

(Contd.)

Beats	Movement	Direction
	The Dwight	
17	With knees bent slightly and weight on balls of your feet, twist to left	○
18	Twist to right	
19	Twist to left	
20	Twist to right	
	Shuffle	
21&22	Shuffle-step forward, right, left, right	⇧
23	Rock forward on left foot	
24	Rock back on right foot	
25&26	Shuffle-step backward, left, right, left	⇩
27	Rock back on right foot	
28	Rock forward on left foot	
	Side Shuffle	
29&30	Shuffle-step sideways to right, right, left, right	⇨
31	Rock back on left foot, turning shoulders quarter turn to left	
32	Step forward on right foot and clap	
33&34	Shuffle-step sideways to left, left, right, left	⇦
35	Rock back on right foot, turning shoulders quarter turn to right	
36	Step forward on left foot and clap	

Beats	Movement	Direction
	Long Leg Shakes	
	(Travel forward with exaggerated leg shake)	
37	Step forward on ball of right foot with right knee turned in slightly	
38	Shake knee out to right	
39	Step forward on ball of left foot with left knee turned in slightly	
40	Shake knee out to left	
41,42	Repeat steps 37 and 38	
43,44	Repeat steps 39 and 40	
	Cross Slap Leather	
45	Step right foot over left	
46	Kick up left boot to left and slap with left hand	
47	Step left foot over right	
48	Kick up right boot to right and slap with right hand	
49	With the right foot still up, do a quick pivot quarter turn to left and brush right foot forward past left foot	
50	Brush right foot back past left foot	
51	Stomp right foot down next to left	
52	Stomp left foot next to right and clap	

Begin again!

☆☆☆☆☆☆☆ *Losin' It* ☆☆☆☆☆☆☆

Scott Lanius, Nashville, USA **Two Wall**

These are the steps as taught by the choreographer, although I noticed dancers in The Wildhorse Saloon in Nashville begin the dance on step 9. Oddly, it seems easier this way but try both and see for yourself.

Beats	Movement	Direction
	Step, Clap, Turn, Clap	
1	Step left foot to left side	⇦
2	Touch right foot beside left, clap	
3	Pivot half turn left on ball of left foot, stepping right foot to right side	◖
4	Touch left foot beside right, clap	
	Left Triple-step, Unwind, Clap	
5	Step left foot to left side	⇦
&	Step right foot beside left	
6	Step left foot to left side	
7	Cross right foot over left	
8	Unwind half turn left, clap	◖
	Right Double Kick, Coaster Step	
9,10	Kick right foot forward twice	○
11	Step right foot back	
&	Step left foot beside right	
12	Step right foot forward	

Beats	Movement	Direction
	Left Double Kick, Coaster Step	
13,14	Kick left foot forward twice	❍
15	Step left foot back	
&	Step right foot beside left	
16	Step left foot forward	
	Step, Hitch, Shuffle, Bump Hips	
17	Step right foot forward	
18	Pivot half turn left on ball of right foot, hitching left knee	◖
19&20	Shuffle forward, left, right, left	⇧
21	Step right foot forward right diagonal, bumping hips right	⇧
&22	Bump hips left. Bump hips right	
23	Step left foot forward left diagonal, bumping hips left	
&24	Bump hips right. Bump hips left	
	Repeat first 8 counts in opposite direction . . .	
25	Step right foot to right side	⇨
26	Touch left foot beside right. Clap	
27	Pivot half turn right on ball of right foot, stepping left foot to left side	◗
28	Touch right foot beside left. Clap	
29	Step right foot to right side	

(Contd.)

Beats	Movement	Direction
&	Step left foot beside right	⇨
30	Step right foot to right side	
31	Cross left foot over right	
32	Unwind half turn right. Clap	

Begin again!

☆☆☆☆☆ Marty's Express ☆☆☆☆☆

Vickie Powell, Clarksville, USA **Four Wall**

Beats	Movement	Direction
	Right Vine	
1,2	Step right foot to right side. Step left foot behind right	⇨
3,4	Step right foot to right side. Tap left heel forward 45 degrees left, snap fingers of right hand	
	Left Vine	
5,6	Step left foot to left side. Step right foot behind left	⇦
7,8	Step left foot to left side. Tap right heel forward 45 degrees right, snap fingers of right hand.	
	Scissors	
&	Cross right foot over left	○
9	Step left foot right to centre	
&	Step right foot to right side	
10	Touch left heel forward 45 degrees left	
&	Step left foot centre	
11	Cross right foot over left	
&	Step left foot to left side	

(Contd.)

Beats	Movement	Direction
12	Touch right heel forward 45 degrees right	
&	Cross right foot over left	
13	Step left foot right to centre	
&	Step right foot to right side	
14	Touch left heel forward 45 degrees left	
&	Step left foot centre	
15	Cross right foot over left	
16	Unwind half turn left	
	Three Kick, Half Turn	
17	Kick right foot forward, snap right fingers	
18	Weight on left foot, turn quarter turn left and kick right foot forward, snap right fingers	
19	Repeat step 18	
20	Pause *(hold right foot in raised position)*	
	Rock Steps	
21	Rock back onto right foot	
22	Rock forward onto left foot	
23	Stomp right foot beside left	
24	Pause	
	Reverse Vine Right	
25	Cross left foot over right, angle body 45 degrees right	

Beats	Movement	Direction
26	Step right foot to right side . . . body centre	
27	Cross left foot over right, angle body 45 degrees right	
28	Swing right foot out to right side, slap right heel with right hand	
	Reverse Vine Left	
29	Cross right foot over left, angle body 45 degrees left	⇦
30	Step left foot to left side . . . body centre	
31	Cross right foot over left, angle body 45 degrees left	
32	Swing left foot out to left side, slap left heel with left hand	
	Cross, Slap, Cross, Slap	
33	Cross left foot over right, angle body 45 degrees right	❍
34	Swing right foot out to right side, slap right heel with right hand	
35	Cross right foot over left, angle body 45 degrees left	
36	Swing left foot out to left side, slap left heel with left hand	

(Contd.)

Beats	Movement	Direction
	Rock Steps	
37	Rock forward onto left foot	
38	Rock back onto right foot	
39	Rock forward onto left foot	
40	Stomp right foot beside left	
	'V' Hops	
41	Hop both feet together forward 45 degrees right	
42	Hop both feet back to centre	
43	Hop both feet together forward 45 degrees left	
44	Hop both feet back to centre	
	Step, Drag, Turn, Stomp	
45	Step left foot forward	
46	Slide right foot up behind right	
47	Step left foot, turning quarter turn left	
48	Stomp right foot beside left	

Begin again!

☆☆☆☆ 96-Step Hip-Hop ☆☆☆☆

Richard Tymko, USA **Four Wall**

Beats	Movement	Direction
	Steps 1–8	
	Chugs (8 beats)	
1–4	Step with left foot 4 times, turning *(in-total)* quarter turn to right *(pivot on ball of right foot)*	◥
5–8	Step with right foot 4 times, turning *(in-total)* quarter turn to left *(pivot on ball of left foot)*	◤
	Steps 9–16	
	Jumping Jacks (8 beats)	
1&2	Jump with feet apart, feet together, feet apart	○
&	Jump, turning half turn right, land feet together	◗
3&4	Jump feet apart, feet together, feet apart	○
&	Jump, turning half turn left, land feet together	◖
5&6	Jump feet apart, feet together, feet apart	○
&	Jump, turning half turn right, land feet together	◗
7&8	Jump feet apart, feet together, feet apart	○

(Contd.)

Beats	Movement	Direction
	Steps 17–20	
	Chugs (4 beats)	
1–4	Step with right foot 4 times, turning *(in-total)* quarter turn left *(pivot on ball of left foot)*	◖
	Steps 21–40	
	Kick-Step-Turn x5 (20 beats)	
1& 2&	Kick left foot forward, step left foot back. Step right foot back, step left beside right	❍
3&4	Scuff right forward, turning quarter turn left, lift right knee, stomp right foot. Repeat pattern 4 more times. End facing original starting wall	◖
	Steps 41–48	
	Vaudeville Steps (8 beats)	
1,2&	Step left foot to left side, step right foot behind left, step left foot to left side	❍
3,4&	Step right foot to right side, step left behind right, step right foot to right side Repeat pattern once more	
	Steps 49–56	
	Running Man (8 beats)	
1	Step right foot forward	

Beats	Movement	Direction
&	Scoot back on right foot, hitching left knee	❍
2	Step left foot forward	
&	Scoot back on left foot, hitching right knee	
3	Step right foot down	
&	Swivel heels left	
4	Swivel heels to centre	
5	Step left foot forward	
&	Scoot back on left foot, hitching right knee	
6	Step right foot forward	
&	Scoot back on right foot, hitching left knee	
7	Step down on left foot	
&	Swivel heels right	
8	Swivel heels to centre	

Steps 57–60

Jump Cross (4 beats)

Beats	Movement	Direction
1,2	Jump feet apart, jump crossing right leg over left	❍
3&4	Jump feet apart, feet together, feet apart	

Steps 61–64

Hops (4 beats)

Beats	Movement	Direction
1	Hop *(feet still apart)* both feet to right	⇨

(Contd.)

Beats	Movement	Direction
2	Hop both feet to left	⇦
3&4	Hop to right, right, right	⇨

Steps 65–68

Pigeons (4 beats)

Travelling left . . .

Beats	Movement	Direction
1,2	Jump with toes pointed out (V-shaped).	⇦
	Jump with toes pointed in (Λ shaped)	
3&4	Jump toes out, toes in, toes out	

Steps 69–72

Window Washer (4 beats)

Beats	Movement	Direction
1	Step right foot back diagonal right	⇩
2	Step left foot back diagonal left	
3	Step right foot back diagonal right	
4	Step left foot forward, clap	

Steps 73–80

Basketball Turns (8 beats)

For every turn, pivot on left foot, push off with right foot . . .

Beats	Movement	Direction
1	Pivot half turn left *(9 o'clock)*	◖
2	Pivot half turn right *(3 o'clock)*	◗
3	Pivot half turn left *(9 o'clock)*	◖
&	Jump, crossing left foot over right	
4	Jump, uncrossing feet	❍

Beats	Movement	Direction
	For every turn, pivot on left foot, push off with right foot . . .	
5	Pivot half turn right *(3 o'clock)*	◗
6	Pivot half turn left *(9 o'clock)*	◖
7	Pivot half turn right *(3 o'clock)*	◗
&	Jump, crossing right foot over left	
8	Jump, uncrossing feet	○
	Steps 81–88	
	Big Steps (8 beats)	
	Shimmy shoulders and upper body . . .	
1,2	Step left foot forward at *(12 o'clock)*	⇧
3,4	Step right foot beside left	
5,6	Step left foot back	⇩
7,8	Step right foot beside left	
	Steps 89–96	
	Electric Kicks (8 counts)	
1	Jump right foot back, kicking left foot forward	○
&	Step left foot back	
2	Step right foot forward	
&	Step left foot forward	
3	Jump right foot back, kicking left foot forward	
&	Step left foot back	
4	Step right foot forward	

(Contd.)

Beats	Movement	Direction
5,6	Walk forward, left, right	⇧
7	Step left foot beside right with toes pointed left	
&8	Spin one-and-a-quarter turn left on left foot, step down on right *(now facing 9 o'clock)*	●

Begin again!

☆☆☆☆ North-Side Cha-Cha ☆☆☆☆

One Wall

Beats	Movement	Direction
	Side Steps and Cha-Cha	
1	Step left foot to left side	⇦
2	Step right foot beside left	
3&4	Cha-Cha on the spot left, right, left	❍
5	Step right foot to right side	⇨
6	Step left foot beside right	
7&8	Cha-Cha on the spot right, left, right	❍
	Cross-Over Rock Steps and Cha-Cha	
9	Rock left foot across right	❍
10	Rock back onto right foot	
11&12	Cha-Cha on the spot left, right, left	
13	Rock right foot across left	
14	Rock back onto left foot	
15&16	Cha-Cha on the spot right, left, right	
17–20	Repeat steps 1–4	
	Rock, Half Turns and Cha-Cha	
21	Rock back onto right foot	❍
22	Rock forward onto left foot	
23&24	Cha-Cha on the spot right, left, right,	

(Contd.)

Beats	Movement	Direction
	turning half turn left	◖
25	Step left foot back	
26	Step right foot forward, turning half turn right	◗
27&28	Cha-Cha on the spot left, right, left	❍
	Diagonal Walk and Cha-Cha	
29	Step right foot diagonally forward	⇗
30	Step left foot diagonally forward *(same direction)*	
31&32	Cha-Cha on the spot right, left, right	❍
	Step Back, Half Turn Right, Cha-Cha	
33	Step left foot diagonally back	⇙
34	Step right foot forward, turning half turn right	◗
35&36	Cha-Cha on the spot left, right, left	❍
	Step Forward, Half Turn, Cha-Cha	
37	Step right foot forward	
38	Pivot half turn left *(now facing original wall)*	◖
39&40	Cha-Cha on the spot right, left, right	

Begin again!

☆☆☆☆☆ Outlaw Antics ☆☆☆☆☆

Knox Rhine, Everett, USA — ***Four Wall***

Beats	Movement	Direction
	Chug, Chug, Out-Cross-Out	
1	Slide left foot 1/8 turn to right	❍
2	Slide left foot 1/8 turn to right	
3	Jump both feet apart	
&	Jump crossing right foot over left	
4	Jump both feet apart	
	Repeat steps 1–4 with right foot leading . . .	
5	Slide right foot 1/8 turn to left	❍
6	Slide right foot 1/8 turn to left	
7	Jump both feet apart	
&	Jump crossing left foot over right	
8	Jump both feet apart	
	Cross, Pivot, Heel-Toe-Cross	
9	Cross right foot over left, bend knees	
10	Pivot half turn left, shifting weight to right foot, straighten knees	◖
11	Tap left heel forward	
&	Step ball of left foot beside right	
12	Cross right foot over left	

(Contd.)

Beats	Movement	Direction
	Repeat steps 9–12 with left foot leading . . .	
13	Cross left foot over right, bend knees	
14	Pivot half turn right, shifting weight to left foot, straighten knees	◗
15	Tap right heel forward	
&	Step on ball of right foot beside left	
16	Cross left foot over right	
	Monterey Spin	
17	Touch right toe to right side	
18	Slide right foot *(as if drawing a circle)* towards left foot. Pivot 1 full turn right, transferring weight to right foot	●
19	Touch left toe to left side	
20	Cross left foot over right, transferring weight to left foot	
21–24	Repeat steps 17–20	
	(Stationary) Roger Rabbits	
&	Lift right foot slightly, scoot forward on left foot	❍
25	Step right foot behind left	
&	Lift left foot slightly, scoot forward on right foot	
26	Step left foot behind right	
&	Lift right foot slightly, scoot forward on left foot	

Beats	Movement	Direction
27	Step right foot behind left	❍
&	Rock forward onto left *(feet still crossed)*	
28	Step right foot in place	
	Repeat steps &25–28 with right foot scoot . . .	
&	Lift left foot slightly, scoot forward on right foot	❍
29	Step left foot behind right	
&	Lift right foot slightly, scoot forward on left foot	
30	Step right foot behind left	
&	Lift left foot slightly, scoot forward on right foot	
31	Step left foot behind right	
&	Rock forward onto right foot *(feet still crossed)*	
32	Step left foot in place	
	Touch, Cross, Touch, Cross	
33	Touch right toe to right side	
34	Cross right foot over left, stepping forward	⇧
35	Touch left toe to left side	
36	Cross left foot over right, stepping forward	

(Contd.)

Beats	Movement	Direction
	Touch, Spin Half Turn, Touch, Together	
37	Touch right toe to right side	
38	Pull right ankle to left knee and spin half turn left	◖
39	Touch right toe to right side	
40	Touch right toe beside left foot	
	Out-Out, Clap, In-In, Clap	
&	Step right foot to right side	❍
41	Step left foot to left side	
42	Clap	
&	Step right foot to centre	
43	Step left foot to centre	
44	Clap	
	Right, Behind, Touch and Touch	
45	Step right foot to right side	⇨
46	Step left foot behind right	
47	Touch right toe to right side	
&	Place right foot beside left *(switching feet)*	
48	Touch left toe to left side	
	Cross, Unwind, Kick-Ball-Change	
49	Cross left foot over right	◗
50	Unwind half turn right	
51	Kick right foot forward	

Beats	Movement	Direction
&	Step on ball of right foot	
52	Step left foot in place	
	Step, Quarter Turn, Kick-Ball-Turn	
53	Step right foot forward	
54	Pivot quarter turn left on balls of feet	
55	Kick right foot forward	
&	Step on ball of right foot beside left, lift left slightly and pivot quarter turn left	
56	Step left foot beside right	
	Jazz Box with Quarter Turn, Point	
57	Cross right foot over left	
58	Step left foot back	
59	Step right foot forward, turning quarter turn right	
60	Point left toe to left side	
	Slap, Point, Slap, Point	
61	Cross left knee in front of right leg, slap with right hand	
62	Touch left toe to left side	
63	Cross left knee in front of right leg, slap with right hand	
64	Point left toe to left side	

Begin again!

☆☆☆☆☆☆ Outta' Line ☆☆☆☆☆☆

Scott Blevins, USA — ***Four Wall***

Beats	Movement	Direction
	Steps 1–4	
	Running Man	
1	Step right foot forward	❍
&	Slide right foot back, lifting left foot	
2	Step left foot down and forward	
&	Slide left foot back, lifting right foot	
3&4&	Repeat steps 1&2&	

Beats	Movement	Direction
	Steps 5–8	
	Stomp, Clap, Step, Stomp, Clap	
5,6	Stomp right foot forward, clap	⇧
&	Step left foot beside right	
7,8	Stomp right foot forward, clap	

Beats	Movement	Direction
	Steps 9–16	
	Cross Step Cross Unwind, Body Rolls	
1	Cross right foot behind left	⇦
&	Step left foot to left side	
2	Cross right foot over left	
3	Stomp left foot beside right	
&	Kick left foot forward diagonally left	
4	Cross left foot over right	

Beats	Movement	Direction
5,6	Unwind half turn right	◗
7,8	Roll body ending weight on left foot	
	Steps 17–20	
	Kick and Dig, Pivot Turn	
1	Kick right foot forward	○
&	Step on ball of right foot	
2	Tap left heel forward	
&	Step on ball of left foot	
3	Step right foot forward	
4	Pivot half turn left	◖
	Steps 21–24	
	Stomp, Scissor Hitch and Clap	
5	Stomp right foot forward	○
&6	On balls of feet twist heels in, out	
&7	Hitch right knee, clap	
8	Step right foot in place	
	Steps 25–28	
	Body Rolls	
1,2	Side moving body roll left *(snake-like from head down to waist)*	⇦
3,4	Side moving body roll right	⇨
	Steps 29–32	
	Heel Jacks	

(Contd.)

Beats	Movement	Direction
&	Jump diagonally back right on right foot	❍
5	Extend left heel forward diagonal left	
&6	Jump feet together first left, then right	
&	Jump left foot back diagonally left	
7	Extend right heel forward diagonal right	
&8	Jump feet together first right, then left	

Steps 33–40

Pivot Turns, Scoot Forward

Beats	Movement	Direction
1	Step left foot forward	◗
2	Pivot half turn right	
3,4	Repeat steps 1,2	
&	Step left foot forward	
5	Step right foot in line with left *(feet shoulder-width apart)*	
6,7	Scoot both feet forward twice with knees bent	⇧
8	Hitch right knee, clap	❍

Steps 41–45

Rolling Right Vine 1 1/4 Turn

Beats	Movement	Direction
1	Step right foot to right side, turning quarter turn right	◗
2	Turn half turn right on right foot, swinging left foot around	◗
3	Turn half turn right on left foot, swinging right foot around	◗

Beats	Movement	Direction
4	Step right foot down	
5	Step left foot in line with right, feet shoulder-width apart	❍
	Steps 46–48	
	Elvis Legs	
6	Pop *(bend)* right knee in towards left leg	❍
7	Pop left knee in *(straighten right leg)*	
&	Pop right knee in	
8	Pop left knee in, ending weight on left foot	

Begin again!

☆☆☆☆☆☆ Rev 'Em Up ☆☆☆☆☆☆

Sandra and Linda Mailman, West Palm Beach, USA ***Two Wall***

If using You Win My Love, *begin the dance when you hear Shania sing 'Come On' to end dance facing front wall.*

Beats	Movement	Direction
	Crossover Steps, Jump Back, Heel Forward	
	Begin with feet shoulder-width apart	
1	Cross left foot over right	❍
&2	Cross right foot over left	
3	Cross left foot over right	
&4	Jump back on right foot, extending left heel forward 45 degrees left	
	Repeat steps 1–4 with right foot leading . . .	
5	Cross right foot over left	❍
&6	Cross left foot over right	
7	Cross right foot over left	
&8	Jump back on right foot, extending right heel forward 45 degrees right	
	Alternate Steps:	
	Steps 1–8 may be danced as a reverse right and reverse left vine	

Beats	Movement	Direction
	Hip Bumps, Half Turn Left	
9,10	Lean on right foot, bump hips right twice	❍
11,12	Bump hips left, twice	
13,14,15	Bump hips right, left, right	
16	Turn half turn left	◖
	Scoot, Crossover	
17,18	Scoot forward twice on left foot, hitch right	⇧
19	Cross right foot over left	
	Shuffle on Spot, Kick Twice	
20&21	With feet still crossed, shuffle on the spot, right, left, right	❍
22,23	Kick left foot twice	
24	Cross left foot over right	
25&26	With feet crossed shuffle on the spot, left, right, left	❍
27,28	Kick right foot twice	
	Paddle	
29	Step right foot forward	
30	Pivot quarter turn left on ball of left foot	◂
31,32	Repeat steps 29,30	

(Contd.)

Beats	Movement	Direction
	Shuffle Diagonal Forward and Back	
33&34	Shuffle forward 45 degrees forward right *(1 o'clock)*, right, left, right	
35&36	Shuffle forward, same direction *(1 o'clock)*, left, right, left	
37&38	Shuffle backward 45 degrees left *(7 o'clock)*, right, left, right	
39&40	Shuffle backward, same direction *(7 o'clock)*, left, right, left	
	Jump, Cross, Unwind, Clap	
41	Jump out with feet shoulder-width apart	
42	Jump, crossing right foot over left	
43	Unwind half turn left	
44	Clap *(feet still shoulder-width apart)*	
	Hip Bumps	
45,46	Bump hips left twice	
47,48	Bump hips right twice	

Begin again!

☆☆☆ The Rock & Roll Waltz ☆☆☆

Max Perry, Danbury, USA **Two Wall**

This is a fantastic 2-part dance – a real challenge but great fun. It must be danced to Scooter Lee, don't try anything else!

Beats	Movement	Direction
	PART A	
	Hesitation Steps Forward and Back	
1	Step left foot forward	⇧
2	Step right foot beside left on ball of foot	
3	Step left foot in place	
4	Step right foot forward	
5	Step left foot beside right on ball of foot	
6	Step right foot in place	
7	Step left foot back	⇩
8	Step right foot beside left on ball of foot	
9	Step left foot in place	
10	Step right foot back	
11	Step left foot beside right on ball of foot	
12	Step right foot in place	
	3 Twinkles, Unwinding Turn	
13	Cross left foot over right *(angle body right)*	❍
14	Step right to right side on ball of foot	
15	Step left foot in place	

(Contd.)

Beats	Movement	Direction
16	Cross right foot over left *(angle body left)*	○
17	Step left foot to left on ball of foot	
18	Step right foot in place	
19–21	Repeat steps 13–15	
22	Cross right foot over left	
23,24	Unwind half turn left	◖

Rolling 360 degrees Left (3-step turn)

Beats	Movement	Direction
25	Step left foot forward, turning quarter turn left	⇦ ◢
26	Step right foot back, turning half turn left	◖
27	Step left foot to left side, turning quarter turn left *(now facing front wall – 12 o'clock)*	◢

Cross-Over Rock Step

Beats	Movement	Direction
28	Rock right foot forward across left foot	○
29	Step left foot in place	
30	Step right foot beside left	

Half Box Turn (Half square 180-degree turn in 6 steps)

Beats	Movement	Direction
31	Step left foot forward, turning quarter turn left *(9 o'clock)*	◢
32	Step right foot beside left on ball of foot	
33	Step left foot beside right	○

Beats	Movement	Direction
34	Step right foot back, turning quarter turn left *(6 o'clock)*	◢
35	Step left foot beside right on ball of foot	
36	Step right foot beside left	○
37–48	Repeat steps 25–36 *End of A . . . 48 steps*	
	PART B ***'One, Two and Let's Rock . . .'*** ***Walk Forward and Rock Hips***	
1	Step left foot forward	⇧
2	Step right foot forward	
&	Step left foot to left side *(small step)*	○
3	Step right foot to right side *(feet shoulder-width apart)*	
4,5,6	Swing hips left, right, left *(end with weight on left foot)*	
	'. . . One, Two and Let's Roll . . .' ***Walk Forward, 3 Step Half Turn***	
7	Step right foot forward	⇧
8	Step left foot forward	
&	Step right foot to right side *(small step)*	
9	Step left foot to left side *(feet shoulder-width apart)*	○

(Contd.)

Beats	Movement	Direction
10	Step right foot forward, turning quarter turn right *(3 o'clock)*	◗
11	Step left foot to left side, turning quarter turn right *(6 o'clock)*	◗
12	Step right foot beside left	
	Walk Forward, Scoot	
13	Step left foot forward	⇧
14	Step right foot forward	
&	Step left foot to left side *(small step)*	○
15	Step right foot to right side *(feet shoulder-width apart)*	
16–18	Scoot forward 3 times	⇧
	Walk Forward, 3-Step Half Turn	
19–24	Repeat steps 7–12	
	Cross-Over Rock Step Left and Right	
25	Rock left foot forward across right *(angle body 45 degrees right)*	○
26	Step right foot in place	
27	Step left foot beside right on ball of foot	
28	Rock right foot forward across left *(angle body 45 degrees left)*	○
29	Step left foot in place	
30	Step right foot beside left on ball of foot	

Beats	Movement	Direction
	Forward Stomp and Present Hand	
31	Stomp left foot left diagonal forward, bending left knee with weight over left foot. Left arm forward, palm up	⇖
32,33	Mark time, tap left heel twice	○
34	Stomp right foot right diagonally forward, bend right knee, weight over right foot. Right arm forward, palm up	⇗
35,36	Mark time, tap right heel twice	○
	Full Box Turn (Square 360-degree turn in 12 steps)	⇧ ⇨
37–48	Performed exactly as the half turn in PART A, steps 31–36	⇦ ⇩
	Repeat second time to complete a full box	
	(You are now facing 12 o'clock)	
	End of B . . . 48 steps	

Commence dancing with the vocals

Dance A twice

Dance B twice

Dance A Once

Dance B Once

Dance will end facing back wall

☆☆☆ Romeo (a.k.a. Redneck Romeo) ☆☆☆

Melanie Greenwood, USA — ***Four Wall***

Beats	Movement	Direction
	Step, Scuff, Quarter Turn Left	
1	Step right foot forward	⇧
2	Scuff left foot forward	
3	Step left foot quarter turn left	◖
4	Touch right foot beside left	
	Quarter Turn Right	
	Turn slightly on next four beats to face 12 o'clock . . .	
5	Pop left knee *(raise left heel)* bump hips right	◗
6	Pop right knee *(raise right heel)* bump hips left	
7,8	Repeat steps 5,6	
	Vine Right	
9	Step right foot to right side	⇨
10	Step left foot behind right	
11	Big step right foot to right side	
12	Slide left foot up to right and hitch *(raise knee)*	

Beats	Movement	Direction
	360-degree Left Turn	
13	Big step left foot to left side	
14,15	Hop on left foot twice, right foot hitched turning 360 degrees left to 12 o'clock	
16	Step right foot down	
	Syncopated Heel, Toe Pattern with Quarter Turn Left	
17	Tap left heel forward	
&	Step left foot in place	
18	Tap right heel forward	
&	Step right foot in place	
19	Tap left toe behind right	
&	Step left foot in place	
20	Tap right toe behind left	
&	Step right foot in place	
21	Tap left toe back	
&	Step left foot in place	
22	Tap right toe back	
&	Step right foot quarter turn left	
23	Tap left heel forward	
&	Step left foot in place	
24	Tap right toe back	
	Rock Forward and Back	
25	Rock right foot forward	

(Contd.)

Beats	Movement	Direction
26	Rock back onto left foot	❍
27	Rock right foot back	
28	Rock forward onto left foot	
	Hip Roll and Bump	
29,30	Roll hips full circle counter-clockwise	❍
31	Bump hips right	
32	Bump hips left	

Begin again!

☆☆☆☆ 2nd Avenue Stroll ☆☆☆☆

Barry Amato, Nashville, USA — ***Four Wall***

Beats	Movement	Direction
	Stroll Forward	
1,2	Cross right foot over left, hold	
3,4	Cross left foot over right, hold	
5	Cross right foot over left	
6,7,8	Unwind full turn left *(weight on right heel and ball of left foot)*	
	Step, Hitch, Turn and Shasay	
9	Step right foot forward	
10	Hitch left leg	
11	Quarter turn to right *(left leg still hitched)*	
12	Step left foot to left side	
13	Step right foot beside left	
14	Step left foot to left side	
15	Step right foot beside left	
16	Step left foot to left side	
	Windmill Turn and Stomp Forward	
17,18	Quarter turn left *(swing right foot forward)*, clap	
19,20	Half turn left *(swing left foot back)*, clap	
21	Stomp right foot forward	
22	Stomp left foot forward	

(Contd.)

Beats	Movement	Direction
23	Stomp right foot forward	⇧
24	Stomp left foot forward	
	Syncopated Steps	
25	Tap right heel forward	❍
&26	Step on right foot, tap left heel forward	
&27, 28	Step on left foot, kick right foot forward twice	
&29	Step on right foot, left toe across right foot	
30	Tap left heel forward	
31	Hitch left leg	
32	Step left foot in place	
	Pivot Turns and Shuffle Forward	
33	Pivot quarter turn right on right foot	◗
34	Tap left toe behind	
35	Pivot half turn left on left foot	◖
36	Tap right toe behind	
37	Step right foot back	
38	Tap left heel forward	
39	Step left foot forward	
&	Lock right foot behind left	⇧
40	Step left foot forward	

Begin again!

☆☆☆☆☆☆ Smokin' Gun ☆☆☆☆☆☆

Debbie Brink, Poway, USA **Four Wall**

Beats	Movement	Direction
	Right Vine and Slaps	
1	Step to right with right foot	⇨
2	Step left foot behind right	
3	Step to right with right foot	
4	Bring left foot up behind right knee and slap boot with right hand	○
5	Touch left toe out to left side	
6	Bring left foot in front of right knee and slap boot with right hand	
	Left Vine and Slaps	
7	Step to left with left foot	⇦
8	Step right foot behind left	
9	Step to left with left foot	
10	Bring right foot up behind left knee and slap boot with left hand	○
11	Touch right toe out to right side	
12	Bring right foot in front of left knee and slap boot with left hand	
	Right Vine	
13	Step to right with right foot	⇨
14	Step behind right with left foot	

(Contd.)

Beats	Movement	Direction
15	Step to right with right foot	
16	Stomp left foot next to right	
	Slide Forward	
17	Step forward on left foot	⇧
18	Slide right foot up to meet left	
19	Step forward on left foot	
20	Bring right foot up behind left knee and slap boot with left hand	
	Slide Back	
21	Step back on right foot	⇩
22	Slide left foot back to meet right	
23	Step back on right foot	
24	Bring left foot in front of right knee and slap boot with right hand	
	Steps and Slaps	
25,26	Step forward on left, slap right boot behind with left hand	❍
27,28	Step back on right, slap left boot in front with right hand	
29,30	Step forward on left, stomp right foot next to left	
31	With weight on balls of feet, split heels apart	
32	Bring heels back together	

Beats	Movement	Direction
	Slide and Turn	
33	Step forward on right foot	⇧
34	Slide left foot to meet right foot	
35	Step forward on right foot	
36	Bring left foot behind right knee, slap left boot with right hand	
37	Step back on left foot	
38	Slide right foot back to meet left foot	
39	Step back on let foot and lift right knee	
40	Slap right knee with right hand	
41	Step forward on right foot, doing a half turn to left and lifting left knee as you come around	◖
42	Slap left knee with left hand	

Beats	Movement	Direction
	Slide and Slap	
43	Step forward on left foot	⇧
44	Slide right foot to meet left foot	
45	Step forward on left foot	
46	Bring right foot behind left knee and slap boot with left hand	
47	Step back on right foot	⇩
48	Slide left foot back to meet right	
49	Step back on right and lift left knee up	

(Contd.)

Beats	Movement	Direction
50	Slap left knee with left hand	
51	Step forward on left foot	
52	Stomp right foot next to left	
53	With weight on balls of feet, split heels apart	❍
54	Bring heels back together	

Begin again!

☆☆☆☆☆ Something Little ☆☆☆☆☆

Sandy Collins & Dorothy Wicks, W. Palm Beach, USA Four Wall

Beats	Movement	Direction
	Out-In, Crosses, Rolling Vines	
&1	Step left foot out to left side. Step right foot out to right side	❍
&2	Step left foot to centre. Cross right foot over left	
&3&4	Repeat steps &1&2	
5–8	Rolling vine left OR vine left, stomp right foot on last count	⇦ ●
&9	Step right foot out to right side. Step left foot out to left side	❍
&10	Step right foot to centre. Cross left foot over right	
&11&12	Repeat steps &9&10	
13–16	Rolling vine right OR vine right, stomp left foot on last count	● ⇨

Beats	Movement	Direction
	Strut, Half Turn/Gallop	
	Moving forward on next four counts	
17	Touch right toe to right side	
18	Cross right foot over left *(bend knees)*	⇧
19	Touch left toe to left side	
20	Cross left foot over right *(bend knees)*	
21,22	Step right forward. Pivot half turn left	◖

(Contd.)

Beats	Movement	Direction
&23 &24	Two gallop steps forward, right, left, right, left *(right hand over head, swing lasso)*	⇧
	Kick-Ball-Changes, Quarter Turn	
25-28	Right kick-ball-change, twice	○
29&30	Step right foot forward. Turn quarter turn left	◖
31&32	Right kick-ball-change	○
	Triple, Rock, Lunge, Stomp	
33&34	Triple-step to right side, right, left, right	⇨
35,36	Rock back onto left foot. Step right foot in place	
37	Lunge to left side on left foot	⇦
38	Slide right foot to meet left	
39,40	Stomp left foot in place. Stomp right foot in place	○
	Forward Hip Bumps, Half Turn, Slide	
41&42	Bump left hip to left twice *(angle body)*	○
43&44	Bump right hip to right twice *(angle body)*	
45	Kick left foot forward	
46	Turn half turn left, stepping down on left	◖
47	Step right foot forward	
48	Slide left toe to right heel *(weight on right)*	⇧

Beats	Movement	Direction
	Heel Jacks	
&49	Step left foot back. Extend right heel forward	❍
&50	Step right foot back in place. Step left foot in place	
&51&52	Repeat steps &49&50	
&53	Step right foot back. Extend left heel forward	
&54	Step left foot back in place. Step right foot in place	
&55&56	Repeat steps &53&54	

Begin again!

☆☆☆☆☆☆ Star Kick 2 ☆☆☆☆☆☆

Two Wall

This can be a two-part dance. Part 1, in the Beginners' section, may be danced as often as liked. An 8-count bridge section, danced once, links the two. Part 2 is danced until the song ends.

Beats	Movement	Direction
	Bridge Section	
1&2	Shuffle forward left, right, left	⇧
3&4	Shuffle forward right, left, right	
5	Step left foot back	
6	Step right foot back	⇩
7	Step left foot back	
8	Step right foot beside left	

Beats	Movement	Direction
	Left Foot Boogie and Monterey Turn	
	Weight on right, twist left foot as follows . . .	
1	Twist toes left	⇦
2	Twist heel left	
3	Twist toes left	
4	Twist heel left	
5	Touch right toe on right side	
6	Make half turn to right *(swing right leg around)* and step right foot beside left	◗
7	Touch left toe to left side	
8	Step left foot beside right	

Beats	Movement	Direction
9–16	Repeat steps 1–8	
	Heel Twist	
	Twist both feet . . .	
17	Toes left	
18	Heels left	
19	Toes Left	
20	Twist onto left heel, making quarter turn right, kicking right foot forward	
	Rock Back and Forward, Shuffle Forward	
21	Rock back onto right foot	
22	Rock forward onto left foot	
23&24	Shuffle forward right, left, right	
	Modified Left Vine, 3 Step Hitches	
25	Step left foot to left side	
26	Step right foot behind left	
	Make a slow three-quarter turn left on next 6 steps	
27	Step left foot to left side	
28	Hitch right knee, turning slightly left	
29	Step right foot forward	
30	Hitch left knee, turning slightly left	
31	Step on left foot *(now facing back wall)*	
32	Hitch right knee	

(Contd.)

Beats	Movement	Direction
	Right Vine	
33	Step right foot to right side	⇨
34	Step left foot behind right	
35	Step right foot to right side	
36	Touch left foot beside right	
	Rolling Left Vine (360-degree Turn in 3 Steps)	
37	Step left foot to left, turning quarter turn left	⇦
38	Swing right leg forward, turning quarter turn left	
39	Swing left leg back, half turn left	
40	Touch right foot beside left, clap	
	Hip Shakes	
41&42	Shake hips to right, twice	○
43&44	Shake hips to left, twice	
	Travelling Pigeon Toes	
45	Twist left toes left, right heel left	⇦
46	Twist left heel left, right toes left	
47,48	Repeat steps 45,46	

Begin again!

☆☆☆☆☆ The Sunflower ☆☆☆☆☆

Four Wall

When learning this dance, keep your kicks and hops simple and later, when you've mastered it, try the variations suggested. It's a dance you'll want to do with enthusiasm!

Beats	Movement	Direction
	Left Vine	
1	Step left foot to left	⇦
2	Step right foot behind left	
3	Step left foot farther to left	
4	Kick right foot and hop on left	
	Right Vine	
5	Step right foot to right	⇨
6	Step left foot behind right	
7	Step right foot farther to right	
8	Kick left foot and hop on right	
9	Hop on left, let right foot swing out a little to side	❍
10	Hop on right, let left foot swing out a little to side	
11	Hop onto left	❍
12	Kick right leg high in front	

(Contd.)

Beats	Movement	Direction
	(or if you are really daring, kick your heels together to the right)	
13	Hop onto right	
14	Kick left leg high in front *(or kick your heels together to the left)*	
15&16	Turn quarter turn to left, triple-step in place *(left, right, left)*	
17&18	Turn half turn to right, triple-step in place *(right, left, right)*	

Begin again!

☆☆☆☆☆ Walkin' Wazi ☆☆☆☆☆

Two Wall

Beats	Movement	Direction
	Heel and Kick	
1	Tap right heel forward	❍
2	Step right foot in place	
3	Tap left heel forward	
4	Step left foot in place	
5,6	Kick right foot forward twice	
7	Step right foot way back	
8	Tap left heel forward	
9	Step left foot down, turning quarter to left	◖
10	Scuff right foot forward	
11–20	Repeat steps 1–10	
	Right Weave	
21	Step right foot to right side	⇨
22	Step left foot behind right	
23	Step right foot to right side	
24	Step left foot across right	
25–28	Repeat steps 21–24	
	Shuffle and Pivot Turn, Stomp	
29&30	Right shuffle step forward *(right, left, right)*	⇧

(Contd.)

Beats	Movement	Direction
31	Step left foot forward	
32	Pivot half turn to right	◗
33	Step left foot forward	
34	Pivot half turn to right	◗
35,36	Stomp left foot twice	

Begin again!

☆ Music Lists ☆

Music suitable for each of the dances featured in this book is listed below. These of course are only suggestions (or the particular song usually danced to) and alternative songs can be chosen.

Beginner Level Dances

Dance	*Artist*	*Song Title*
Back in Trouble	Mark Chestnutt	Trouble
Badly Bent Charleston	The Tractors	Badly Bent
Belt Buckle Boogie	Tim Mc Graw	Down On The Farm
Bubba 2	Shenandoah	If Bubba Can Dance (I Can Too)
Chocolate City Hustle	The Mavericks	Excuse Me
CMT County Jamming Strut	Ricochet	Daddy's Money
Country Boy	BR5-49	Cherokee Boogie
Cowgirl Twist	Delbert McClinton	Why Me?
Earthquake	Ronnie Milsap	Earthquake
Electric Slide	Brooks & Dunn	Little Miss Honky Tonk
The Florida Love Bug	Mary Chapin Carpenter	The Bug
The Freeze	Kevin Sharp	If You L:ove Somebody
God Blessed Texas	Little Texas	God Blessed Texas
The Grundy Gallop	John Michael Montgomery	SOLD
Guitar Boogie	Wynonna	Girls with Guitars
Harpoon Stomp	Shenandoah	Darned If I Don't...
Hillbilly Rock, Hillbilly Roll	The Wool packers	Hillbilly Rock, Hillbilly Roll
Hog Wild	Hank Williams Jr	Hog Wild
Honky Tonkin'	Travis Tritt & Marty Stuart	Honky Tonkin's What I Do Best
Honky Tonk Stomp	Joe Diffie	Honky Tonk Attitude
Honky Tonk Twist 2	Sam Cooke	Twistin' The Night Away
Hooked on Country	Atlantic Pop Orchestra	Just Hooked On Country Part 1
Norma Jean	Diamond Rio	Norma Jean Riley
Out with a Bang	David Lee Murphy	Out With A Bang
Redneck Macarena	The Groove Grass Boyz	Macarena
Reggae Cowboy	Bellamy Brothers	Get Into Reggae Cowboy

Dance	*Artist*	*Song Title*
Rockin' the House	Lee Roy Parnell	If The House Is Rockin'
Rocky Top	Osbourne Bros	Rocky Top
Ski Bumpus	George Strait	Blue Clear Sky
South-side Shuffle	Ray Kennedy	What A Way To Go
Star Kick	Shania Twain	I'm Outta Here
Swing City Jive	Roger Brown & Swing City	Swing City
Symphony Shuffle	Rodney Crowell	Let The Picture Paint Itself
The Tall T	Alan Jackson	Tall Tall Trees
Texas Twist	Joe Diffie	Prop Me Up Beside The Jukebox (If I Die)
Trashy Women	Confederate Railroad	Trashy Women
Tulsa Time	Little Texas	A Night I'll Never Remember
Twelve Step	Hal Ketchum	Mama Knows the Highway
Valley Rock	Little Texas	Down in the Valley
The Watermelon Crawl	Tracy Byrd	Watermelon Crawl
The Wrangler Wrap	George Strait	Check Yes or No

Intermediate Level Dances

Dance	*Artist*	*Song Title*
All Aboard	The Dean Brothers	My Baby Thinks She's A Train
All Shook Up	Elvis Presley	All Shook Up
American Pie	Just Luis	American Pie
Arumba	David Lee Murphy	Out With a Bang
Big Ole Truck	Toby Keith	Big Ole Truck
Black Coffee	Lacy J Dalton	Black Coffee
Breakin' the Bank	John Anderson	Money In The Bank
Bubba	Shenandoah	If Bubba Can Dance (I Can Too)
Bump in the Dark	Janet Jackson	If
The Cajun Queen	George Strait	Adalida
The Cajun Slap	Mary Chapin Carpenter	Down At The Twist & Shout
California Coast	Bellamy Bros	Dancin' Cowboys
Caribbean Cowboy	Buster Poindexter	Hot, Hot, Hot
Cha-cha Maria	Brooks & Dunn	My Maria

Dance	*Artist*	*Song*
Church Street Station Stomp	Tanya Tucker	Already Gone
Cimmeron Boogie	Hal Ketchum	Sure Love
The Cinderella	Garth Brooks	It's Midnight Cinderella
CMT's Dance Ranch Romp	Twister Alleyl	Dance
Cotton Country Queen	Ron Wallace	Cotton County Queen
Countdown Shuffle	Jimmy Collins	Rodeo Rock
The Cow Boogie	Clay Walker	Boogie Till The Cows Come Home
Cowboy Hand Jive	Smokin' Armidillos	I'm A Cowboy
Cowboy Rhythm	BR5-49	Little Ramona...
Crazy Legs	Hank Williams Jr	Hog Wild
Cruisin'	The Beach Boys	Still Cruisin'
Daddy's Money	Ricochet	Daddy's Money
Dancin' Hearts	Tracy Lawrence	I See It Now
The Dizzy Cowpoke	Confederate Railroad	Notorious
Elvira	Oak Ridge Boys	Elvira
Emilio Shuffle	Emilio	Even If I Tried
Firecracker	Brooks & Dunn	You're Gonna Miss Me When I'm Gone
Foot Boogie	Kevin Sharp	Population 4000 Minus 1
Four Star Boogie	George Strait	Adalida
Good Ol' Boys	Jimmy C Newman	Rhinestone Cajun Rides Again
The Grundy	John Michael Montgomery	Sold (Grundy County Auction Incident)
Hawaiian Hustle	Ronnie Milsap	Earthquake
Hit Kick	Alan Jackson	Gone Country
Hold Up!	Ronna Reeves	Rodeo Man
Howlin' at Midnight	Neal McCoy	Hillbilly Rap
Interchange	Shania Twain	No One Needs To Know
The J Walk	Tracy Byrd	Walking To Jerusalem
Jo T. Jam	Wynonna	Rock Bottom
José Cuervo '97	Kimber Clayton	Jose Cuervo
Just for Grins	Billy Dean	That Girl's Been Spying On Me
Kelly's Cannibals	Mark Knopfler	Cannibals
Kickin' Country	Confederate Railroad	All I Wanted
LA Walk	Radney Foster	Just Call Me Lonesome

Dance	*Artist*	*Song*
Las Vegas Strut	Garth Brooks	Two Of A Kind Workin On A Full House
Linda Lu	Lee Greenwood	Linda Lu
Line Dance Crazy	Sean Kenny	Line Dance Crazy
Lonestar Shuffle	Lonestar	No News
Lost in Texas	Asleep At The Wheel	Boogie Back To Texas
Louisiana Hot Sauce	Scooter Lee	He's My Little Jalapeno
Make Mine Country	Tracy Byrd	Honky-Tonk Dancing Machine
Midnight Waltz	The Mavericks	Children
Moonlight Waltz	Tracy Lawrence	Stars Over Texas
My Maria	Brooks & Dunn	My Maria
One Step Forward	Desert Rose Band	One Step Forward
Ooh! Aah!	Hanzel Martinez	Love Potion #9
Psycho Cowboy	George Jones	Hi-Tech Redneck
Rattlesnake Shake	Rick Tippe	Rattlesnake Shake
Ridin'	The Rednex	Ridin' Alone
Rock Around the Clock	Brother Phelps	Anyway The Wind Blows
Rock It	The Tractors	Baby Likes To Rock It
Rockin' Rebel	Collin Raye	That's My Story
Rodeo	Carlene Carter	Every Little Thing
Romeo	Dolly Parton	Romeo
Rompin' Stompin'	Scooter Lee	Rompin' Stompin'
Six Shooter	Marty Stuart	If I Ain't Got You (Club Mix)
Slappin' Leather	Travis Tritt	T-R-O-U-B-L-E
Smokey Places	Ronnie Mc Dowell	Smokey Places
The Snakebite	Aaron Tippin	There Ain't Nothin' Wrong With The Radio
Swamp Thang	The Grid	Swamp Thing
Tennessee Twister	Dwight Yoakam	Guitars, Cadillacs
Texas Twister	Brookes & Dunn	Heartbroke Out of My Mind
Thin Sole Shoes	George Jones	Hi-Tech Redneck
The TL Shake	Tracy Lawrence	If The Good Die Young
Tobacco Boogie	Hank Williams Jr	Tobacco Road
Tropicana Parking Lot	Lee Roy Parnell	You're Taking Too Long
Tush Push	Wynonna Judd	Tell Me Why
Vancouver Boogie	Brooks & Dunn	Boot Scootin' Boogie
Walkin' the Line	Kentucky Headhunters	Only Daddy That'll Walk The Line

Dance	Artist	Song
Waltz Across Texas	John Michael Montgomery	Dream On Texas Ladies
'X'ed Out	Emilio	Even If I Tried

Advanced Level Dances

Dance	Artist	Song
Achy Breaky Heart	Billy Ray Cyrus	Achy Breaky Heart
Ain't Goin' Down	Garth Brooks	Ain't Goin' Down...
Applejack	Garth Brooks	Callin' Baton Rouge
Arlene	Dan Seals	Bop
Back In Your Arms	Lorrie Morgan	Back In Your Arms
Chaos	Joe Diffie	Third Rock From The Sun
Charlie's Sidekick	Rhett Akins	What They're Talkin' About
Cowboy Hip Hop	Wynonna	No One Else On Earth
Electric Reel	*Lord of the Dance*	Cry of the Celts (Track 16)
Foot Loose	Brooks & Dunn	My Maria
GMC	The Real McCoy	Ooh Boy
The Honk Tonk Twist	Scooter Lee	The Honky Tonk Twist
Hot Tamales	Lee Roy Parnell	Country Down To My Soul
Indian Runner	Tim Mc Graw	Indian Outlaw
Kickin' It Up	John Michael Montgomery	Kickin' It Up
Kneel Hail	Brett James	Female Bonding
Le Doux Shuffle	Little Texas	Kick A Little
Long-legged Hannah	Jesse Hunter	Long Legged Hannah...
Losin' It	Kevin Sharp	Measure Of A Man
Marty's Express	Marty Stuart	Honky Tonk Crowd
96-step Hip-Hop	Pam Tillis	Shake The Sugar Tree
North-side Cha-cha	Garth Brooks	Friends In Low Places
Outlaw Antics	Garth Brooks	Callin' Baton Rouge
Outta' Line	Shania Twain	I'm Outta Here
Rev 'Em Up	Shania Twain	You Win My Love
The Rock & Roll Waltz	Scooter Lee	The Rock & Roll Waltz
Romeo	Dolly Parton	Romeo
2nd Avenue Stroll	Tim Mc Graw	I Like It, I Love It
Smokin' Gun	Confederate Railroad	Queen of Memphis
Something Little	John Nelson	A Little Something
Star Kick 2	Shania Twain	I'm Outta Here
The Sunflower	Clinton Gregory	Hacksaw
Walkin' Wazi	Carlene Carter	I Fell In Love

☆ Choreographer Credit ☆

Choreographers who have kindly granted permission for their dances to appear in this book include:

Barry Amato
c/o Susan Charney & Associates
212 3rd Ave No. Suite 301
Nashville TN 37201
USA
ph: + 615 254 4208
fx: + 615 254 4308
e-mail: rockinhorse@sprynet.com

Debbie Brink
Western Boot Scootin'
13619 Fairgate Dr
Poway CA 92064
USA
ph: + 619 679 1586

Max Perry
163 South Street # 84
Danbury,
CT 06810
USA
ph: + 203 798 9312
fx: + 203 744 4552
web site: www.maxperry.com

Hillbilly Rick
R2 Box 150A
Haubstadt
IN 47639
USA
ph: + 812 867 3401
fx: + 812 867 1082
e-mail: hillbillyr@aol.com
web site: www.hillbillyrick.com